Early Educator's Tool Box

The Guide to Early Learning Materials and Program Application

Pamela Tuchscherer

Pinnaroo Publishing

To my patient children: Jamie, Holly and Todd

ISBN: 0-939705-01-X

Pinnaroo Publishing
P.O. Box 7525
Bend, Oregon 97708

Printed in the United States of America

Production: Tyson Tuchscherer

Although the author has exhaustively researched all sources listed in this book to ensure accuracy, completeness and their extended availability, she assumes no responsibility for inconsistencies such as change of price or availability which may occur.

Table of Contents

Introduction

Discovering good resources and learning how others successfully apply them is my goal as editor of a national newsletter for early childhood educators. Now, after two years, numerous conferences and hundreds of phone calls later, I have over 100 discoveries I'm excited to share with you.

Remember, even the best teacher needs the right tools for the job. Use the following pages as your reference. Just pick your topic and learn of practical programs and resources that can motivate students and make teaching easier. Many have specific ideas for successful application from teachers who use them. Some, particularly in the health and safety sections, contain vital information that could protect young lives.

As an early childhood educator, I know you enjoy discovering new things, so do read through sections that at first may not suit your immediate needs—What color is a tiger beetle anyway? (SCIENCE)

All the programs and resources were chosen for their practicality, quality and reasonable price. I have listed the source of the materials so you can order directly to the publisher, with a couple of exceptions. These are books which may be obtained through interlibrary loans. Simply ask your school, city or county librarian about their interlibrary loan programs that makes almost any book that has been published, available from libraries around the country.

There are many useful teaching strategies included within the articles dealing with the nurturing of personal and social development of young children. These, in addition to the materials and resources I have included, can be used in a variety of ways—integrating them into the classroom curriculum or in the creation of new and exciting programs.

I would like to thank all the organizations, large and small, which have assisted me in providing the information and illustrations included in this book. Please see illustration credits at the end of the book.

Classroom Activities

For teachers seeking a variety of activities throughout the year, Children's Television Workshop has two books available, **Sesame Street Activities** and **Sharing the Street: Activities for All Children.**

Activities from Big Bird and Friends

Both books, aimed at preschoolers, link the content of Sesame Street with learning activities—reinforcing the educational goals presented on the program. The books are available for $2.50 each.

The activities in **Sesame Street Activities** (65 pp.) are grouped into five sections: "The Child & His World," "Using Symbols," "Learning Skills," "Bilingual/Bicultural," and "Sesame Street Instructional Goals."

Common word and number matching and rhyming games are supplemented by those utilizing imagination, experimentation and problem-solving. Occasional activities incorporate such characters as Big Bird, Oscar and Cookie Monster which adds new flavor to familiar games.

Reprinted with permission by Children's Television Workshop. Copyright 1986 Children's Television Workshop. Copyright 1986 Muppets, Inc.

Sharing the Street (96 pp.), created for individuals working with children who have special needs as well as other young children, contains a broad selection of sensory experiences important to every child's development. Each activity contains learning skills and sensory stimulation. Some provide the children with "practice and diversified experience in using their senses," while others are designed to help children learn to understand and appreciate the differences among people. "Big Bird's Radio Station," "Oscar's Trash Can Garden," and "The Broken Letter Shop," are a sample of the 42 activities—many of which include adaptations for children with disabilities.

To order **Sesame Street Activities** and **Sharing the Street**, send request and remittance payable to:

Children's Television Workshop
Community Education Services Division
Dept. A-1
One Lincoln Plaza
New York, NY   10023

It started with an agate that Donny brought to class. Now you have a whole collection of rocks and shells. How can you help your students learn more about these natural objects and find other well-tested activities appropriate for them?

Learning Activities

The book, **Activities for the Young Scientists** (#17, $8), includes a chapter on rocks and shells and is designed for use with 4-year-olds. The 55 activities presented in this booklet provide a variety of discovery and observational experiences.

This is only one example of the many early education materials created by the Ferguson-Florissant School District Early Education Program. Their mailing brochure, available free of charge on request, divides the available materials into three sections: Activity Ideas for Teachers; Activity Ideas for Parent and Child; and Programming with a Dual Focus: Parent and Child.

Each item listed includes a description and a recommended age level, covering a range from birth to Kindergarten-Grade One. Some examples are:

Learning Activities for Threes (#7, $13.50) Contains some 300 sequenced activities in Language, Math, Cooking, Fingerplays, Art, Fine and Gross motor. Helpful for any child working at the 3- or 4-year-old level, as well as those with developmental lags for problems. Each activity on a separate page of easy reference.

Skill and Concept Checklist from Birth through Five (Revised 1986, #9-$5) The basis for planning a curriculum—contains separate check sheets for each age and lists sequentially the specific skills and concepts to work toward in the following areas: Motor, Language, Math-Science, Social Skills, and Self-help.

The programming section contains material directed toward administrative tasks and include such titles as:

Evaluating a Preschool Program (#45, $2.50) Samples of instruments developed to measure effectiveness of staff and program.

Putting Together a Staff Development Program for Preschool Teachers (#47, $2).

Materials ordered from the Early Education Department which total less than $25 must be prepaid. Add $4 for shipping and handling for orders $12 and under. To receive more information on ordering large quantities, write to:

Early Education Program
Ferguson-Florissant School District
1005 Waterford Drive
Florissant, MO   63033
(314) 831-8809

Hands-on experiences in the early childhood classroom can range from playing with play dough and puzzles to using a large variety of educational toys. One of the basic tools, the cookie cutter, now comes in a large variety of shapes.

Shaping the Imagination

In the play area and in the cooking center, children seem never to tire of rolling dough and creating figures with cookie cutters. If you're ready to replace or supplement your cookie cutter collection, and can't find a local supplier, you can order excellent Norpro cutters from Kitchen N' Things in Seattle. Choose between airplanes, dolphins, turkeys, locomotives, sailboats and more, all available by mail.

Shapes available for 59 cents each:

Pear (F3330)	Owl (F3319)
Hand (F3344)	Cross (F3320)
Ice Cream Cone (F3350)	Car (F3322)
Alligator (F3351)	Mushroom (F3328)
18 Wheeler (Truck) (F3370)	Apple (F3329)
Guitar (F3371)	Whale (F3331)
Strawberry (F3374)	Sailboat (F3333)
Swan (F3376)	Locomotive (F3334)
Dinosaur (F3383)	Cat (F3336)
Seahorse (F3402)	Elephant (F3339)
Umbrella (F3403)	Donkey (F3340)
Giraffe (F3405)	Pig (F3341)
Maple Leaf (F3407)	Eagle (F3344)
Unicorn (F3408)	Butterfly (F3345)
Coffee Pot (F3409)	House (F3347)
Kangaroo (F3411)	Church (F3348)
Tow Truck (F3414)	Foot (F3349)
Cow (F3415)	Teapot (F3352)
Ship (F3417)	Dolphin (F3355)
Seashell (F3363)	Chick (F3357)
Rocking Horse (F3364)	Number 1 (F3391)
Airplane (F3372)	Number 2 (F3392)
Pineapple (F3375)	Number 3 (F3393)
Fire Hydrant (F3379)	Number 4 (F3394)
Rabbit (F3307)	Number 5 (F3395)
Dog (F3310)	Number 6/9 (F3396)
Duck (F3311)	Number 7 (F3397)
Turkey (F3312)	Number 8 (F3398)
Cardinal (F3313)	Number 0 (F3390)

To order, send quantity, item number, description, price of each item and total price. Shipping charges for orders totaling up to $9.99 add $1.95; $10 to $19.99 add $2.95; $20 to $29.99 add $3.95. Washington residents add 7.9% sales tax. Send order and remittance to:

Kitchen N' Things
2322 NW Market Street
Seattle, WA 98107

Looking for an alternative to competitive games—which often eliminate young children from the activity? Below is a resource which may fulfill your needs.

Don't Wake Up the Grump

Many times competitive games cause players to feel separated and "left out" and the play becomes secretive, rather than open. Hurt feelings or arguments often result. If this sounds familiar and you are looking for an alternative to your game corner, consider the **Sleeping Grump**.

This fascinating game has a strong emphasis on cooperation and can be played by a small group at activity time. In the game, the Old Grump has taken the villagers' treasures and is now fast asleep at the top of the beanstalk. Together, players climb the stalk and recover their treasures. Grump must not be awakened, or he will take back everything. Best of all, players share the treasures and always leave some behind for the Grump.

The game contains a board (6"X24"), markers, tokens, rules and "no frills" box. The game is best suited for kindergarteners, however 4-year-olds who know their colors and numbers could play it easily after some initial guidance.

Sleeping Grump is worthwhile for those interested in initiating a cooperative game corner where children can find that it is mutually beneficial to help one another so that everyone can win. Once the children gain experience at this game, they can work together to develop other games with a cooperative concept.

To request a free catalog, write to:

Animal Town Game Co.
P.O. Box 2002
Santa Barbara, CA 93120

Ask an early childhood teacher if she has a computer or would like one in her classroom and you will probably get an enthusiastic "yes," or an emphatic "no." The following articles give some of the reasoning behind these two opposing views.

Alternatives to a Computer

A new item on the budget list of many early education programs is the computer. However, there are divergent opinions about how and when it should be introduced to children.

Are computers good for kids? "No, not necessarily so," according to Dr. Joseph Weizenbaum, professor of computer science at the Massachusetts Institute of Technology. "There are many, many other ways to learn about the world than using computers."

Weizenbaum believes having children "master their own language"—both through speaking and writing, and learning to appreciate their natural and cultural environment are priorities that have been neglected.

The use of computers may also serve to inhibit or cover up questions that should take place, Weizenbaum said. If a child is having trouble learning a skill, the use of a computer can allow a teacher to give the child practice, but not address the problem of why the child is not learning.

James Hoot, assistant professor of early childhood education at North Texas State University in Denton, also believes computers have disadvantages, and discussed them in his article, "A Computer for Children: Don't worry if you don't have one," (**Texas Child Care Quarterly**, Vol.8,No.2). One objection is the expense. By purchasing a computer, a school or center may possibly deprive the staff of increased salaries and much needed materials, he said. He is also concerned with the quality of some software available and the developmental shortcoming of written directions given to non-reading 3-to-5-year-olds.

Land crabs versus keyboards

Like Dr. Weizenbaum, Hoot says there are many alternative ways to allow children to learn new skills. Instead of using the computer to compare and match objects, generate colors, and create shapes, he suggests using real objects such as rocks or beads, paper and crayons, and playdough. For fostering eye-hand coordination, a high level of motivation or a sense of control—all points stressed in the positive use of computers—Hoot suggests such activities as sewing cards, land crabs in a terrarium or hammering nails into wood.

For those interested in introducing computer concepts, an alternative to an expensive computer system could be a "computer play center." Such a center was developed by Theresa Rubens, Jennifer Poole and Hoot, and described in "Introducing Microcomputers to Micro Learners Through Play," (**Day Care and Early Education**, Vol.11, No.4). In addition to common keyboards from calculators, typewriters and donated computer terminals, the center included computer paper, tape recorders with computer sounds, pictures of people using computers and robot dress-up clothes.

Computer play center

If you are interested in ideas on how to set up a computer play center, The Corporate Child Development Fund has a well-illustrated, four-page "Computer Play Center" plan available for $1. It includes a description of various activities and plans for a computer model, circuit and monitor.

To order, send request and remittance to:

The Corporate Child Development Fund
510 So. Congress, Suite 122
Austin, TX   78704

Computers as a Learning Tool

"We promote and encourage block building, not for children to learn to be carpenters, masons or architects. We have cooking in the classroom, not for children to learn how to cook. We introduce the typewriter, not for the children to learn typing. In all these instances, the activity instead is a learning tool to help children develop in the areas of physical, cognitive, language, social, emotional, and creative growth. It is the same with the computer. This tool is especially powerful in promoting social skills...if you set up your learning center properly," Janice Beaty writes in the draft for her forthcoming book, **Computer as a Paintbrush** (C. Merrill, 1987), which she co-authors with W. Hugh Tucker.

Turn-taking, turn-waiting and helping each other occur if more than one child is allowed to use the computer at one time, according to Beaty who is also associate professor of Human Sciences at Elmira College (NY). As an active participant in child-computer studies and a researcher, she has found that the use of microcomputers will cause young children to become socially isolated only if the teacher sections off the computer area and allows only one child at a time to use it.

17

Allow two children to work together

"Instead, we suggest that teachers take advantage of the drawing power of this unique new learning tool and allow two children to sit at the keyboard at one time. A few others can watch and comment. Let the two users work out their own turns [they use self-regulating devices such as computer necklaces] and their own methods for using the various programs," she said.

Exploring their options freely and playfully in order to discover how the computer works allows children to learn that it does more than print letters and show pictures.

In the chapter, "The Computer as a Playmate," there is an excellent description of how the Elmira Computer Project selected a computer program, utilized it in the classroom, and integrated it into the classroom curriculum.

Their program choice was "Jeepers Creatures"(Kangaroo Incorporated). A mix-and-match animal game, which shows a picture of an animal that is divided into three parts horizontally, was chosen because it can be used successfully at the beginning of a computer program with preliterate children.

The head, the body and the feet are controlled by the top, middle, or bottom of a particular row of keys on the keyboard. The child presses any one letter on the keyboard and something will happen. Children are able to mix up heads and bodies and feet of animals such as a kangaroo, a panda bear, an octopus, a cat. There are three different "zoos" of 10 animals.

Select programs based on your personal previews

"Another program might have been just as satisfactory," Beaty said. "Whatever program you choose for your own children should be based, first of all, on your personal preview of the program."

Consider, also, your objectives for the children when selecting programs. Beaty and her co-workers' objectives were that the program would:

1. Involve children in a simple but interesting learning game.
2. Have simple, nonverbal directions.
3. Allow children to learn how to play on their own without difficulty.
4. Have a graphic appear on the screen for any key pressed.
5. Be a first step in a sequence of programs, each of which would build on the children's skills learned in the previous programs.*

As the children used "Jeepers Creatures," some would push keys and look up at the monitor screen—figuring out the rules of the program. Others pressed one key after another without looking up—showing they did not understand the correlation between the key and the screen.

"With two children at the keyboard, however," Beaty said, "a great deal of peer teaching occurred."

Once the children had an opportunity to manipulate the keyboard and master the program, the "experts" invented new ways to use a graphic, press a key, or touch the monitor, Beaty said. They invented new games, such as making names and sounds for the animals they created.

Another reason "Jeepers Creatures" was selected was for the ease of integration into the preschool curriculum. "It is essential that the computer become an integrated part of the curriculum," Beaty said. The computer should be located near other activities and the programs should have counterparts and follow-ups in other activity areas.

Let the computer become a stimulus in the classroom

For example, with "Jeepers Creatures" a teacher can make available a related activity such as a "Crazy Animal" card game which has mix and match pieces. Reading books about strange animals and turn-taking, and giving children the opportunity and material to make up their own "curious creature" stories, are other suggested activities.

"Let the computer be a stimulus in your classroom for all sorts of new experiences for the children," Beaty said.

For teachers considering a computer in the classroom, or for those who already have that tool available, Beaty's book should be an informative and practical resource to add to the bookshelf. (This book is due to be published in January 1987).

*Reprinted by permission from **Computer as a Paintbrush** by Janice Beaty and W. Hugh Tucker, (C.Merrill, 1987).

Missing Toy Parts

Don't discard toys and games if they are missing simple parts. Many corporate toy makers will charge little or nothing to replace these parts. Just provide the toy maker with the specific toy name or a brief description of the part you would like replaced.

CBS Toys, 41 Madison Ave., New York, N.Y. 10010. 212-683-7810.

Coleco Industries, Customer Service, P.O. Box 460, Amsterdam, N.Y. 12010. 518-843-4873.

Creative Playthings, See address for CBS Toys.

Empire of Carolina, P.O. Box 427, Tarboro, N.C. 27886. 9190823-4111.

Fisher Price, 620 Girard Ave., East Aurora, N.Y. 14052. 1-800-828-1440.

Gabriel-Child Guidance, See address for CBS Toys.

Hasbro, Customer Service, 1027 Newport Ave., Pawtucket, R.I. 02862. 1-800-556-6997.

Ideal, See address for CBS Toys.

Kenner Products, 10114 Vine St., Cincinnati, Ohio 45202. 1-800-543-7073.

Lauri, Inc., Phillips-Avon, Maine 04966. To obtain Lauri replacement pieces, send a stamped, self-addressed envelope and 50 cents handling fee per piece; $1 for puzzle frames. Include a description of the piece, and the piece or puzzle frame color.

Little Tikes, 8705 Freeway Dr., Macedonia, Ohio 44056. 1-800-321-0183.

Mattel Toy Division, 5150 Rosecrans Ave., Hawthorne, Calif. 90250. 1-800-421-2887.

Ohio Art, P.O. Box 111, Bryan, Ohio 43506. 419-636-3141.

Parker Bros., 190 Bridge St., Salem, Mass. 01970. 617-927-7600.

Remco, 1107 Broadway, New York, N.Y. 10010. 212-675-3427, ext. 241.

Tonka Toys, 4144 Shoreline Blvd., Spring Park, Minn. 55384. 612-475-9500.

Reprinted by permission from **Child's Play**, USA Toy Library Association, 1800 Pickwick Ave., Glenview, IL 60025.

Art

Enhance Perceiving Powers

You've just returned from a walk outside and Jonathan, having noticed the new spring leaves overhead, wants to draw a tree. He sits down, thinks for a moment and then comes over to ask, "I don't know how to draw a good tree. Will you help me?"

Many children, especially those who have spent a great deal of time coloring in color books or tracing pictures, hesitate to draw certain objects for fear they will not turn out the way "they're supposed to look."

One way to widen children's vision and show them that there are many acceptable ways to draw objects is to introduce them to a variety of art. This exposure can be through books, games, pictures and reproductions. In **The Arts and Human Development** (Wiley, 1973) Howard Gardner explains it's possible to improve perceiving powers of children as early as nursery school because of their sensitivity to the fine aspects of visual arts through continual observation.

Children's perception is also affected by their daily experiences, and their physical and cultural environment, which results in individual preferences. Because these preferences and the children's discrimination capabilities change frequently, it is important to allow exposure to a large variety of pictures. The more they come in contact with visual art, the more they begin to see past the immediate appearance and begin to cultivate their powers of perception.

The styles of art to choose from are unlimited. Examples of everyday experiences and portraits can include works by Andrew Wyeth, Norman Rockwell, Picasso, Renoir and Mary Cassatt. There are landscapes by Monet; figurative pieces by Degas; and, of course, work from other cultures such as Oriental scrolls and African prints.

Things aren't always normal

Many children enjoy abstract paintings more than realistic ones because of their different style and pretty colors. Carolyn Mitas, a visiting teacher at Sunshine Cooperative Preschool (Dallas, OR), likes to challenge the children and have them look at things in a new way. Among the pictures she displays around the room are reproductions by Marc Chagall, an early 20th century painter. "I like to emphasize to the children," she explains, "that things don't always have to be normal. Chagall's paintings of dreams and other works often show an abnormal perspective."

For those interested in a children's book which contains a large variety of abstract and imaginative works, along with a pleasant story, I recommend **Going for a Walk with a Line—A Step into the World of Modern Art** by Douglas and Elizabeth MacAgy (Doubleday, 1959).

Pictures and reproductions, which are copies of original pieces of art, are available in many forms. Some teachers have made books and wall displays with pictures from magazines such as **Smithsonian** and **American Artist**.

The back cover of the **Reader's Digest** is another excellent source of art works. This page is often a detailed portion of a painting, tapestry, batik or other form of art. My children enjoy scanning through the pages of a photo album, where we keep these appealing reproductions, often making up stories as they go.

To add variety, Green Tiger Press (La Jolla, CA) reproduces pictures from old children's books and places them on notecards. Some of the notecard series are titled: "Beatrix Potter Series", "Bears and Teddies", "Cooper Eden Series", "Flower Fairies of Cicily Barker", and "Friendship".

For those who enjoy pictures from childhood, fairies and teddy bears, these pictures reinforce Bryan Holme's feeling, "We feel close to a picture when the subject is familiar and the way it is painted is the way we would love to have painted it if we could, but at other times how exciting it is to find an artist's flight of fancy carrying us, as if on a magic carpet, to an enchanted world we never imagined before." (**Enchanted World—Pictures to Grow Up With**, Oxford University Press, 1980.)

These hand-crafted notecards are attached on a separate piece of high-grade paper. The procedure offers an effect similar to the matting of a print. They are folded to a standard size (5"x7") and come with an envelope. The cards range from $1.25 to $1.50. A free catalog can be obtained by writing, Green Tiger Press, 1061 India, La Jolla, CA 92101.

Reproductions are also available from local book stores and shops as well as from national printing houses and museums. One I have found very useful and economical is the **National Gallery of Art** (Washington D.C.). For $1 you can receive a 43-page catalog of available reproductions. It includes an extensive collection of color reproductions and graphics (11"x14") for 50¢ each; matted reproductions (mat size 14"x18") for $5 and large reproductions (22"x28") for $7.50.

There is a minimum order of $2 plus a $2 handling charge. It is noted also that educational and religious institutions are eligible for a 20 percent discount on orders of more than $10. If you wish to request a discount you are asked to include a purchase order. To order, write to:

Publications Services
National Gallery of Art
Washington D.C. 20565

"Art activities are particularly significant for preschool children because they combine the children's developing ability to use symbols with their persistent desire to handle materials," according to Merle B. Karnes, author of **Creative Art for Learning**. "Few other subjects give children as many opportunities to actually manipulate the materials and to express their own ideas and emotions—the goal of the art curriculum."

The following three books are designed to enhance children's exploration, manipulation and experimentation with art.

Creative Art for Learning

"Have you ever made your own paint brush?"

This is an interesting question to ask your students. You will find that many children have not given much thought to this tool, even though they have used one a number of times.

Creating a paint brush is one of 60 activities found in **Creative Art for Learning**, by Merle B. Karnes. The activity begins by first introducing the three parts of a brush (the handle, the bristles, and the part that holds the bristles to the handle). The children are then given an opportunity to pick up and examine a collection of straw, small twigs, green grass, popsicle sticks and wire—all of which can be used to make a brush.

After the children have manipulated and felt the different textures of the material, they can create their own brush with the help of the teacher (if necessary). Once the odd array of brushes is assembled, the children use their tools to make one brush stroke on a piece of paper using paint or ink. When they have finished, they can all display their papers. The group can look at each of the brush strokes and compare the variety of lines. Drawing a picture of their choice with their brush concludes the activity. *

All of the activties in the book are designed to enhance exploration, manipulation and experimentation. They have been found appropriate for use with handicapped and non-handicapped children from ages 3 to 12. The activities are divided into three basic areas: Exploratory activities, designed to encourage children to examine their environment and stimulate their memory; Art activities, containing specific lessons listing materials, possible concepts, skills involved, suggested activity topics, time allowance and demonstration/procedures; and Activity Topics that suggest subjects for art activities and include dialogue and lists of materials to use.

Be aware of developmental stages

As within other areas of early childhood education, there are developmental stages in an art curriculum. Within the lessons, Ms. Karnes has done a fine job of incorporating the psychology of preschool art with the normal development of young children. For example, if some of the children experience difficulty describing the materials used to make the brushes, she recommends labeling the things as they touch them or rephrase their descriptions: If a child describes something as bumpy, you could say, "Yes, it feels bumpy and rough doesn't it."

There are some painting and sculpturing (art) activities included which may be difficult for young children. Yet, by being aware of developmental stages and selecting those activities aimed at the child's ability, a teacher can provide guidance for a successful experience. I recommend the book for teachers seeking ways to extend their students' creative expression.

To order, send request for No. 192-**Creative Art for Learning** and remittance of $8 (CEC Members $6.80). Orders for $10 or less must be prepaid by check. Institutions should accompany credit orders with purchase order or voucher number.

The Council for Exceptional Children
1920 Association Drive, Dept. CS85
Reston, VA 22091-1589

Art Through Nature

"There is no right or wrong way for children to accomplish a particular art project. Creativity, enhanced through the use of color, shape and texture of natural materials should be the primary emphasis," suggests Jane A. Kane in her new book, **Art Through Nature**.

Unique art activities such as "Farm Animal Food Collage," "Leafy Easel Painting," and "Corn Cob Printing," are introduced, as well as many familiar nature art projects. Each of the 40 activities are highlighted by a large black-and-white photograph and include: an objective, materials, discussion ideas, procedure, suggestions, and a place for notes. There are also suggested readings at the end of each chapter.

"Nature Paints," an activity which helps children learn that color in plants is real and that it can be removed to be used as paint, is an enjoyable fall activity.

Although organized on a seasonal format, Kane notes selected activities can be used when suitable materials are available. To extend the use of leaves in the classroom, there are directions for both a temporary and a permanent leaf press.

Provide ample time for children to explore an art activity—encouraging them to handle and examine the natural materials available, Kane said. Also, allow the child to tell you when they have completed an art project, and try to refrain from asking— "What are you making?" By doing so, you can help promote the child's inventiveness and self-confidence.

Field trips are fun anytime of the year. Stimulating natural curiosity and gaining an aesthetic appreciation of nature are only two of many reasons for taking children out-of-doors. With this in mind, Kane has included a special field trip section.

Art Through Nature, available for $14.95 plus $2.75 for shipping and handling, is a handy resource which allows you to have nature art activities at your fingertips. To order, send the name of the publication and remittance to:

Learning Publications, Inc.
P.O. Box 1326
Holmes Beach, FL 33509

Bringing Art Work to Life

The education staff at the High Museum of Art (Atlanta, GA) has published a **Handbook for Guides** which is based on questioning, "dialogue" and games.

The games are used to facilitate the involvement of the child with a work of art. "Through these games he can respond, imitate, and identify with the colors, the shapes, objects, and spaces—the elements of design in a work of art. He can act out the relationships, formal and otherwise, in a painting or sculpture, thereby analyzing and physically experiencing the work of art, bringing the work to life."

Encourage kids to listen closely

"Soundscapes" is an example of one of the games which ask that kids use themselves and their voices to make sounds. The game should be used carefully, sparely, briefly, and with a goal clearly in sight. (Please note there are activities in this book which are for use with older children.)

General rules: Arrange a small group of students side by side in a crescent in front of a work of art. The size of the group is governed by the size and complexity of the work. Have the group lean forward (hands on knees), study the work for a moment, and close their eyes. Then, one by one, they begin to make sounds, "releasing" the sound of the artwork. You might want to control the order by touching: "When I touch your head, begin making your sound." Encourage the kids to listen closely and slowly build the soundscape. Don't play very long on one painting, and follow up immediately with dialogue; "What was that sound you were making? What made you sound like that?" Or have them open eyes and repeat their sounds one by one as they indicate what in the artwork prompted that sound. Then, put the sounds together again.

This game can be played with realistic or abstract works. If the group is too large to play all at once, split the group. After one team works, have the other do a soundscape. If the kids are doing well, playing fully, and noticing things, split the group again and do four soundscapes at one: "Ready? Begin. Slow and quiet. Gradually build up your soundscape." Or, if you want to make a hunt game, have one team close their eyes while the other makes a soundscape. Then have the "blind" team open up and find the work.*

Handbook for Guides is available for $15, plus $1 for postage and handling from the High Museum of Art. For more information or ordering, write:

Pamela Bray, Curator of Education
Student Programs
High Museum of Art
1280 Peachtree St., NE
Atlanta, GA   30309

*Reprinted by permission from **Handbook for Guides**, High Museum of Art.

Stamping Around with Sponges

Looking for new material to use in the art center? Some interesting and easy-to-use foam sponges are available that can lead children on an artful adventure.

The sponges come in a variety of shapes and sizes including: teddy bears, fruits, sea shells, butterflies and holiday themes. They are just the right size for small children's hands with individual pieces ranging in size from ½" to 5".

Children can dip the forms in water base paint and use them for pattern making or a variety of different art activities. The sets are priced from $5.75 and up, depending on the number of pieces in the kit.

For more information write:

The Great Wallflower Company
21296 Seasprite Circle
Huntington Beach, CA   92646

Nutrition

Nutrition education can be approached in a multitude of ways. Children can learn to identify food by color, shape, taste and smell. They can also experience new cultural food patterns, initiate planting projects and help prepare simple snacks.

Another important aspect of nutrition education is sharing objectives of the program with parents and encourage them to participate as partners in the learning process. This continuity in the approach to nutrition can help children develop sound food habits and contribute to a healthier childhood. Two programs which encourage this positive approach to nutrition education are the **Early Childhood Nutrition Program** and **Food...Early Choices.**

Tiny Bites Begin Discoveries

With recipe cards set up and fruits and vegetables ready to go, the children began creating their own salads. As they sliced and gathered the ingredients they began talking about the croutons and sunflower seeds as if they were choosing toppings for ice cream sundaes. Joe tasted his first kiwi fruit, Becky ate her first lima bean and Tricia discovered how to tackle an artichoke.

Trying new food is often successful in a group setting, for a child may eat something unfamiliar simply because friends are doing it. Having a casual attitude toward eating new foods is best. "When children learn that they will not be forced to eat any food, they will feel more like trying it," suggests Jill Randell and the co-authors of the **Early Childhood Nutrition Program** distributed by Cornell University.

Frequent exposure to new food also increases the chance that children will learn to like the food. "When a new food is introduced, a child may choose to only look at it, or just pick it up and feel it, which is fine. The natural curiosity of children is a benefit when new foods are tried. The next time the food is served, the child may take a tiny bite," the authors say.

The success in handling the introduction of new food, eating habits and other nutritional lessons are shared with parents in the **Nutrition Activities: Preschoolers and Parents** booklet of the kit. For each unit there is an information sheet, a recipe and three activity sheets to complement the classroom experience.

Change the vegetable, not the child

When dealing with vegetables, which seems to be the least liked food among preschoolers, it is often not the vegetable itself the child objects to but the form in which it is served, its texture, or strong taste, the authors point out. As one nutritionist put it, "Try changing the vegetable, not the child."*

Making vegetable sticks (kebabs) with dip, a vegetable delight (drink) or broccoli pancakes, are some options suggested.

The **Early Childhood Nutrition Program** is available for $20. It includes:

The **Nutrition Handbook**—Containing basic nutrition and background information on preschooler's food habits, and resources (52 pages); **Educator's Guide: Food Experiences for Young Children**—An idea and resource book containing the how and why of food nutrition education programs and four activity sections, recipes, ideas for puppets, songs, stories, and resources (190 pages); **Nutrition Activities: Preschoolers and Parents**—An activity book containing information for parents, recipes and activity sheets. (The camera-ready sheets are designed to be duplicated by photocopying).

Other materials available separately are:

Parents and Preschoolers: A Recipe for Good Nutrition—A flip chart of 11" X 17" black-and-white photographs with suggested dialogue and discussion questions and answers (Spanish dialogue included) (15 pages); The **Nutrition Activities:Preschoolers and Parents** ditto book in Spanish, and a lightweight paper booklet version in both English and Spanish.

For more information or ordering the **Early Childhood Nutrition Program**, write to:

Distribution Center
7 Research Park
Cornell University
Ithaca, NY   14850

*M.E. Lowenberg. "Food preferences of young children," **Journal of the American Dietetic Association**, #24, 1948.

Food...Early Choices

What did Chef Combo tell you today?

Chef Combo is a new friend at Discoveries Preschool and helps Barbara Wood, director, introduce nutrition concepts to her class. Barbara purchased Chef Combo—a hand puppet—as part of the **Food...Early Choices** nutrition learning system created by the National Dairy Council.

She feels the system is excellent. "The children look forward to seeing Chef Combo and often ask where he is. They talk to him about things that are going on and enjoy listening to him talk about food."

Some of the areas he discusses are: where food comes from; what food gives us go power and helps us grow strong and healthy; how to be clean and careful when working with food; and most of all, that food tastes good. The children become "food-tasters" and participate in simple food preparation.

Wood, who has a home economics background, feels it well worth the cost because the program is very well done. "The objectives are clear, lessons are easy to follow and the materials can be used over and over. The take-home handouts are a key to parent interest."

The program includes:

A program overview. Teachers Guide (32 pp. including creative suggestions; patterns for learning tools; general nutrition primer; etc.); 25 learning activity cards; Chef Combo Nation hand puppet; 100 food picture cards; Two decks of 36 food-laying cards, Two-sided floor mat; Growing up poster; Where and How we get our food booklet; 16 two-piece food puzzles; Record containing three songs; and 18 duplicating masters to be used as take-home materials to parents.

The major goal of the system is to provide positive experiences which encourage wise food choices by preschoolers and the adults with whom the children interact. The learning activities also contribute to the child's social, emotional, motor, sensory, cognitive, and language development.

For more information, or ordering, contact your local Dairy Council or write to:

National Dairy Council
6300 North River Road
Rosemont, IL 60018-4233

Good Health Tips

There is a wide variety of useful materials available from the National Dairy Council. Planning a health lesson? Your students can see their growth patterns with the aid of the **Growth Record** (#0003), a six-page booklet that discusses foods needed for growth and good health and includes bar graphs where height and weight can be charted.

This is only one example of the reasonably priced materials directed toward children from ages three to seven by the Council, a nonprofit organization devoted to nutrition research and education.

For those interested in dental health there is a poster and miniature poster **Do You?** Both come with teacher guide and focus on the importance of regular toothbrushing, visits to the dentist, and proper food for dental health (Poster #0529) (Miniature #0044).

Another poster-miniature set, **Every Day Eat the 3-2-4-4 Way!** illustrates the Four Food Groups and helps children understand the kinds and amounts of foods needed each day (Poster #0515, Miniature #0021).

A set of four colored posters, **Meals and Snacks for You**, pictures children eating nutritious meals. They are designed to encourage discussions of wise food selection and have a four-page teacher guide listing other activities (#0523).

You can also obtain two portfolios of 12 full-color photographs (11"x14"), with teacher guides on the back of each. **We All Like Milk** (#0002) illustrates baby mammals, alone or with their parents.

If you live in an area where there is a local Dairy Council you should request an order form or materials from them. Each state Council sets its own price on materials it sells. If you are not served locally, contact:

National Dairy Council
6300 North River Road
Rosemont, IL 60018

Letting children cook in the classroom is exciting, but often requires extra attention on the part of the teacher. To make this job easier, there are two cookbooks that are very helpful and supply single portion recipes to be prepared by the children. They also include many helpful hints on how to make the cooking process a fun and successful activity.

Recipes for Independent Learning

Letting children cook in the classroom is exciting, but often requires extra attention on the part of the teacher.

A special cookbook which simplifies this activity is **Cook and Learn** , by Beverly Veitch and Thelma Harms (Addison-Wesley). It contains pictorial step-by-step instructions for 160 single-portion recipes. The recipes vary in difficulty from easily made "Fruit Salad," to more involved "Graham Cracker Apple Pie." There are also multicultural treats such as "Bunuelos."

Many older kindergarteners can follow the recipe straight from the book. Preschool children, however, do best when there is a one-to-one picture correspondence—where the ingredients and measuring tools are placed in front of the recipe cards. They can then walk around a table "reading" and following recipe instructions with little or no adult help.

For teachers who are short on time for printing single-recipe pictures, there is **Recipe Step**, a tablet that includes ready-to-use enlarged steps for 50 favorite recipes from **Cook and Learn** and 20 reproducible parent newsletters. The newsletters contain nutrition and cooking information as well as a "Talk About Page," that includes a recipe to try at home, and discussion starters. To help children organize information and make comparisons, the starter questions suggest that parents might ask their child, "In what ways are pancakes and muffins alike and in what ways are they different?" In this way the child can also learn to recognize relationships.

Time to ask stimulating questions

"By utilizing this type of cooking program, teachers have time to ask stimulating questions and provide interesting follow-up activities rather than spend their time repeating directions," Veitch and Harms said. They say another advantage is that parents and other volunteers can be oriented very quickly to the activity they will supervise.

The cookbook also includes cooking hints, such as beating each egg used with 1 teaspoon of water for easier measuring, as well as such fun activities as setting up a camping environment at school with a repast of hand-made trail mix.

One of the most beneficial aspect of the program is that the children enjoy the feeling of independence and accomplishment when they have completed a recipe. They are then able to take these self-help skills home and be proud of the fact that they are "big enough to help."

The **Cook and Learn** books can be purchased at most educational stores or ordered from:

Addison-Wesley Publishing Company
Jacob Way
Reading, MA   01867
1-800-447-2266

"Crunchy Bananas"

Crunchy Bananas is a well organized and easy-to-follow cookbook for teachers of young children. With the help of preschool teachers, Barbara Wilms has planned and tested recipes chosen for their ease in preparation, children's taste appeal and nutritional value. The selection of recipes varies from basic cut-and-serve salads to ethnic dishes such as "Hot Dog Wonton."

The introduction is filled with valuable insights on cooking—describing its application to various areas of the curriculum such as math, science and prereading. Since young children enjoy being actively involved in the process of learning, Wilms incorporates lessons on time allowances, safety and the selection of the use of equipment.

Prepare for cooking

"Perhaps the most important thing an adult can bring to cooking with children is his patience," Wilms said. "Messes will happen." Some suggestions to take under consideration when preparing for cooking are:

—Never leave a potentially dangerous situation.
—Separate the cooking areas from the preparation area.
—Avoid overcrowding the work space.
—Allow plenty of time.
—Practice play such as beating soapy water, measure rice and stir it up with water

"Another pitfall to avoid is trying to cram in as many recipes as possible to keep children's interest up and build on knowledge and skills," Wills notes. Give them a chance to repeat recipes and master skills like cracking eggs. "A master egg-cracker wants to show off his expertise with endless eggnogs," she said.

Merging the cooking experience with storybooks can be easily done with such books as "Stone Soup" or "The Carrot Seed." Make carrot cake after reading "The Carrot Seed," and the impact of a cooking lesson lingers on.

Crunchy Bananas is available for $5.95. If you mention you read about **Crunchy Bananas** in **Early Educators Tool Box**, you will receive a 10 percent discount. Shipping and handling is $1.50 for the first book and 75¢ each additional book. (California residents add appropriate tax for specific area.)

To order, send name of publication and number (ISBN 0-87-905-507-3) to:

Gibbs M. Smith
Order Department
P.O. Box 667
Layton, Utah   84041

Introducing children to nutritional concepts is also the goal of the book, **Menu for Mealtimes**. It provides a selective list of picture books and coordinated activities to spark children's imagination.

"Menu for Mealtimes"

You are going to visit the bakery next week and you "just know" you've read a good book on bakeries, but you can't think of the title.

By looking up "bakery" in a new booklet, **Menu for Mealtimes**, you might find that book was **In the Night Kitchen** where—"In his dream, Mickey ventures into the night kitchen and helps the bakers prepare the dough for the mornings bread."

Menu for Mealtimes is a bibliography which provides a selective list of picture books and coordinated activities. Each story is annotated and a suitable age range is indicated.

Sandra Feinberg and her coauthors have done a fine job of dividing up the storybook and activities for easy reference. The sections include: Where Food Comes From; Food & Growth; New Foods..Happy Experiences; Breakfast..a Nutritional Bonanza; Snacks..Yes or No?; Food & Manners; Weight Control; Let's Celebrate; Advertising and Your Child's Food Choices; and Potpourri.

Also included are listings of nutritional references and books to extend activities with children as well as a separate index for the authors, titles, subjects and activities.

The booklet, which resulted from coordinated effort between the Librarians Alliance for Parents and Children (Suffolk Co., N.Y.) and the Dairy Council of Metropolitan N.Y., is available by sending $2.50 (make checks payable to Middle Country Public Library) to:

Children's Services Department BIBLIOS
Middle Country Public Library
101 Eastwood Boulevard
Centereach, N.Y.   11720

Science

Come With Me

"Thunder, Thunder, Thunder is what you hear,
When the mighty Brontosaurus suddenly comes near."

These words were chanted by a group of stomping "dinosaurs" at the Community Presbyterian Preschool in San Juan Capistrano, California. Sandra Hillstrom-Svercek, the director, finds her children get totally involved with this activity, which is part of a **Come With Me-Preschool Science Set.**

There are three such sets: Dinosaurs/Reptiles and Amphibians; Sea Animals/Mammals of the Woods; and Insect/Birds. Each includes:

> A tape cassette with ten songs; Two location games which reinforce location words (beside, between, on top of, etc.) plus familiarization with simple addition and subtraction facts or colors; Ten large illustrations of each animal in the set; basic facts of the animals; Art projects, rhythms and creative dramatic activities.

Hillstrom-Svercek has used these science kits for six years with her preschool classes, starting with mature 3-year-olds. She utilizes the teaching pictures, placing them at the children's level for viewing. She has found there is plenty of information which allows for the extension and development of visual perception and other areas of learning.

"Math concepts explode," she continues. "We measure ourselves and compare it to the size of a dinosaur's mouth. We also paint our foot print and compare it with the length of a Tyrannosaurus Rex tooth. The children love it."

The "Come With Me" Science Series was created and developed in the classroom of Pat Perea, who has an extensive background in teaching, music and the use of resource materials for young children. Pat has based the series on the conviction that science is not an isolated subject and can be integrated into other curriculum areas, where student involvement can be a key to learning.

Betty Migliore, a teacher in the Santa Maria (CA) School District, feels the sets are an excellent way to involve science in the classroom. Because the subjects deal with real-life objects, the children can use the material to explore different aspects of these natural creatures.

"It's also easy to incorporate other materials, such as National Geographic pictures into the program," adds Migliore. She also notes that teachers in the district have used other "Come With Me" Science Sets developed for use with kindergarten and older students and have found them a valuable teaching resource.

Come With Me-Preschool Science Sets are available for $10 each plus $1.50 for handling and postage. (CA resides add 6 percent tax, Canadian residents using Canadian funds add 20 percent.)

For more information write or send order to:

S/S Publishing Co.
3550 Durock Rd.
Shingle Springs, CA 95682

Why is it that most of the animals brought into your classroom are insects?

"Insects not only make up 70 percent of the animal kingdom, but also live at the level at which small children do most of their observations," said Marlene Nachbar Hapai, instructor and curriculum writer at University of Hawaii at Hilo.

She suggests helping children understand and appreciate our world's insects by discussing how insects can be beneficial and harmful—including which ones should be avoided. Also assist them in discovering the main body parts and making comparisons.

Three useful books for early childhood classrooms dealing with insects **and** young children follow:

What Color is a Tiger Beetle?

A useful resource to use with children fascinated with insects is **Coloring Fun with Insects** (Entomological Society of America, 1983). A variety of common North American insects is represented to aid children with insect identification and familiarity. Although the society states they are planned for children aged 7-10, I have found them appropriate for 5-year-olds, and even fun to share with older 4-year-olds.

The book contains 46 large, line drawings of insects, coded with numbers for coloring each one as it appears in nature. In addition the insect's name, home or habits, in large print, complements each entry. It is an enjoyable and fascinating summer project for children interested in learning more about their insect friends.

Coloring Fun with Insects is available for $3. To order, send request and remittance to:

Director of Membership Services
ESA
4603 Calver Road
College Park, MD 20740

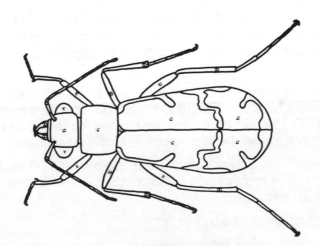

Where Have All the Insects Gone?

As winter approaches, some of the children may begin to question why there are fewer moths, grasshoppers, or beetles around. Although this is not generally a time to study insects, it can be fascinating for children to learn about the seasonal habits of these creatures.

After introducing the fact that insects can be in the larvae or egg stage, have the children think about where they might look for them. Will they be out in the open or hidden away? Discuss why insects might need to hide, (from harsh weather and predators) and how birds might help us find insects (by watching where they look for food).

A rotten log can be a gold mine

Outfitted with warm clothes, plastic bags or containers and possibly a magnifying glass, send the students out to search for the local insect population. They will enjoy searching behind shutters, under loose bark and piles of leaves. A rotten log could be a gold mine of activity.

Don't forget those odd-looking growths on oak trees or the stems or branches of plants. Inside these "galls" could be insects or collections of eggs. (The galls are often formed when an insect lays its eggs on or in the plant, and gives off a chemical that affects the growth of the plant, creating a snug home for the eggs.)

Teachers who don't mind fitting rubber gloves over their woolen ones can scoop mud from the edge and bottom of a pond or stream and take it to the classroom. There the students can place it in a strainer, run water over it, and possibly find dragonfly larvae or whirligig beetles.

For a complete description of these and other winter collecting activities, I recommend the book, **Into Winter—Discovering A Season**, by William P. Nestor. It is available for $9.70 plus $1 for shipping and handling. To order, send remittance and name of publication to:

Houghton Mifflin Co.
Wayside Rd.
Burlington, MA 01803

Creepy Crawlies

An excellent resource for learning more about insects is the book, **Creepy Crawlies—Insects and Other Tiny Creatures**. It illustrates the variety of eating mechanisms possessed by invertebrates in terms young children can understand. The pictures compare the butterfly's feeding tube to a party blower; the grasshopper's jaws with a pair of pliers; the female mosquito's piercing "nose" to a syringe; and the mouthparts of a fly to a sponge.

Your students can also learn that crickets hear with their "knees" (where there is a special opening); flies have suction pads on their feet; and earthworms have tiny bristles on each segment so they can grip the soil as they move about.

This book, a part of the Usborne First Nature Book series, contains beautifully detailed illustrations in full color, which encourages children to explore the lives of many fascinating animals. It is a great resource for teachers who have "insect lovers" in their classroom.

Creepy Crawlies is available for $2.95 plus $1 shipping and handling. To order send remittance and name of publication to:

E.D.C. Publishing
P.O. Box 470663
Tulsa, OK   74147

Can you list five ways in which you can be kind to animals in your neighborhood?

Within most communities the Humane Society can help children answer that question. They have staff members and programs available to help local preschool and kindergarten teachers incorporate humane education into the school's program.

Look...Love...Leave

Llona Robinson, education coordinator for the Humane Society in Bend, Oregon, has found that to help ensure a humane attitude the children first need to understand their place in nature and their responsibility to maintain and care for all life. "We strongly believe that a child who loves and respects nature, will also love and respect others and themselves," she said.

All living creatures need protection

"Protecting an Egg," is an activity she suggests for teachers of young children. The objective is to understand that all living creatures need protection and care from danger. Each child is given an uncooked egg and then allowed to choose an animal sticker and place it on the egg. The teacher explains that everyone needs to be very gentle and protective and be responsible for their egg.

When they have taken care of their egg for a designated time the teacher can ask the children how it felt to be responsible for something so delicate. They can also discuss how human and animal parents must feel about caring for their children. (This activity from: **A Humane Education Curriculum Guide, NAAHE**)

The National Association for the Advancement of Humane Education (NAAHE) has a wide selection of material available for teachers. Two examples are:

Sharing Sam—A Flannel Board Pattern Kit (HE1008)

This kit explains pet care and pet owner responsibility, and includes patterns for making Sam (the dog), his pet care supplies, and props to tell his story; a teaching guide including ideas for vocabulary, spelling and phonics lessons; and a read-aloud story about Sam's life. Each kit is $4 or $3 for NAAHE members.

100 Ways to Be Kind to Animals poster

This free poster lists 100 ways you can be kind to pets and wildlife in your community. Send a SASE (#10-large business size) to **Kind News Poster** to the address below.

For ordering or obtaining information on other available materials write:

NAAHE
Box 362
East Haddam, CT 06423

If You Have a Duck

Another humane education resource is **If You Have a Duck—Adventures to Help Children Create a Humane World** by Jean McClure Kelty. This fascinating 104-page book is about learning to share the earth with animal friends. It is sensitively written and offers insights into the world of animals— both companion and free. It suggests creative, inexpensive projects for understanding animals through humane treatment. Children learn such lessons as why it is important to leave birds' nests alone and what it means to be a social insect—"Social insects live in groups and they help each other. In this way, the ant is like the bee. And both are like people—or like people are supposed to be. We should try to help others all we can, just like the bee and ant."

Many of the activities can be used with 4-and-5-year-olds, however it would be of total use to those who also work with older children. All will benefit from Kelty's message of "Look...Love...and Leave."

To order **If You Have a Duck**, send $9.95 (Ohio residents add 5 percent, in Canada add $1) to:

George Whittell Memorial Press
3722 South Avenue
Youngstown, Ohio 44502

Children are fascinated with all animals including those from the sea. A useful and informative book that deals not only with the animal life of the seashore, but also the water, sand and boats found there, is **Seashore Curriculum Unit**.

 # It's a Unit of Fun

If shells and the seashore are of interest to your students, a book that can help develop this interest into a unit of fun activities is **Seashore Curriculum Unit** by Patricia Stillwell.

This practical resource is useful for teachers with access to the seashore and those who are landlocked. Prepared for the Bay Area Association of the Education of Young Children (Corpus Christi, TX), the activities included were developed by teachers familiar with objects and wildlife unique to the seashore environment.

There are activities which give a general introduction to the seashore as well as sections on water, sand, shells, fish and boats. Each activity relies on child exploration and involvement and suggests an appropriate age level: 18 months and older; 2 and older; 3 and older; 4 and older; and 5 and older.

With activities ranging from making sand and sailboats to tide demonstrations, you can find something of interest for everyone in the class. You can discuss with children who live inland the fact that shell animals such as clams may be found in lakes or rivers, Stillwell said. "The fresh water clam looks like his cousin, but doesn't like salt."

This well-planned book includes not only those "Concepts" or ideas about the seashore that children can understand, but supplies "Adult Facts" so that you have the information needed to teach the concepts.

When studying fish, Stillwell recommends visiting the store to check if they stock shrimp (with feelers and legs), or oysters or crabs still in their shells. Children find it fascinating to touch and explore creatures from the sea.

New meanings to flags and whistles

The chapter on boats introduces children to a variety of ocean-going boats and supplies the teacher with patterns to make cut-outs of the vessels. Learning how boats move and communicate to each other, gives new meaning to flags and whistles.

A list of "Things You Need,""Words to Use," and "What To Do," are described in simple terms. In addition, there is a "Want To Do More" section for each activity which can include songs, fingerplays, and poems which can be found in the "Resource" section at the end of the book. Throughout the 40-page book there are line drawings which illustrate the activities and objects found on the seashore.

An enjoyable and extremely helpful book, **Seashore Curriculum Unit**, is for teachers who want to explore this special seashore environment with their students.

To order **Seashore Curriculum Unit**, send a check or money order for $8, made out to Bay Area AEYC to:

Seashore Curriculum Unit
Pat Stillwell
453 Williamson
Corpus Christi, TX   78411

Moving from live animals, to a small brown creature with large ears, brings us to two energy programs available to classroom teachers from the Energy Source Educational Council and the National Energy Foundation.

Offalot is Watching

The children sit intently as a little brown creature comes up next to the teacher and scans the room. Who is this odd looking puppet with large eyes and ears and what is he looking for?

The children in Carol Hagino's class can tell you. It's Offalot, and he's looking and listening to see if energy is being wasted.

Offalot, the mascot of an energy program managed by the Energy Source Education Council (a non-profit industry-education partnership), introduces kindergarten children to basic concepts such as: people use energy from food to move, speak and think; and cars, home furnaces and vacuum cleaners use energy. Through discussion, the use of picture cards and activity books, children learn how to recognize home energy users and identify ways to save energy and money. Learning to stay away from appliances that burn or cut, and being careful around electrical outlets and old refrigerators are some of the safety lessons also included.

"The children love the puppet, song and picture card activities," Ms. Hagino said. "The last two years when I taught kindergarten here at Birney Elementary (Redondo Beach, Calif.), I used the whole program including the workbook. This year with a combination Kindergarten-1st grade class, I center on the puppet and large picture cards. I find all the children love to get involved with the stories," she said.

"The program lends itself to other parts of the curriculum," Ms. Hagino continued. "Last year, I included it with fire prevention week and also used it in conjunction with a unit on wind energy."

Also throughout the year, the children share what they learn with their families. This sharing is reinforced through the home activity booklets which suggest ways for parents and children to discuss and apply the energy knowledge at home.

"Last year, one of our volunteer mothers came in and explained that her son always used to run outside or to his bedroom to play without turning the television off, much to the disapproval of her husband and herself," Ms. Hagino said.

Children recognize home energy users

Then one day his father had to rush off to work and he left the TV on. "Wait till I tell Dad!" her son said. "You know, if we left the TV on until he got home, we would have a giant energy bill."

"You know," the mother said. "If you hadn't taught him about energy, he never would had given it a second thought."

"The information the children learn is definitely transferred home from the classroom," Ms. Hagino said.

The **Offalot** materials are packaged in three forms: the Teacher pack ($18) contains the teacher guide, hand puppet, set of 20 energy user cards, story picture cards and class poster, "Energy Conservation and Safety"; the Student Pack ($25) contains a record sheet, 35 copies of consumable 16-page student booklets, Home Activity booklets and "I'm an Offalot" badges; and the Class Pack ($39) that includes both the teacher and student materials in a single box. The Home Activity Booklets are also available in Spanish ($5), packaged in sets of ten.

Throughout much of the country, there are business and industry sponsors who provide Energy Source materials to the schools. This can also include private day care and kindergartens, Teanna Boscon, the Council's program administrator said. Teachers interested in learning if there is a sponsorship program in their area should contact Ms. Boscon at the address below.

Teachers can order materials directly, if no industry sponsorship is available in their areas.

For more information or ordering, write to:

> The Energy Source Education Council
> Program Distribution Office
> 5505 E. Carson Street, Suite 250
> Lakewood, CA 90713

Sponsored Program Saves Energy

For those teachers, pre-school through third grade, interested in a useful and exciting energy program there is the **Mini Volts and Wastey Watts Kit** and the **Natural Gas Storybook Kit**, published by the National Energy Foundation. These two kits are available free to teachers in corporate sponsored service areas, through participation in NEF's teacher inservice programs. The inservice programs vary from 3 to 4 hour workshops to college courses for credit, depending on the needs of the educator.

The Mini Volts and Wastey Watts kit covers a variety of energy concepts including: energy sources, electrical safety, energy and water conservation, energy efficiency, personal insulation and food as energy.

The kit contains a storybook which introduces such lively characters Mini-Volts, Wastey Watts and the Glurp. A 60-page lesson plan-teacher's guide filled with activities, energy safety flash cards, energy source flash cards, colorful cut-out bulletin board characters, and finger puppets is included. Each lesson also includes a take-home idea.

One of the program's strengths is the excellent array of activities for various learning levels. The teacher chooses which are applicable to her students. Children can make wind chimes, dress their own cut-out energy doll with different outfits (supplied in the kit), and even construct a play house which is energy efficient with plastic covered windows. Reinforcing energy saving concepts at home is another part of the program's goals.

The "Natural Gas Storybook" kit is another exciting program which focuses on teaching children about an energy source they cannot see hear or smell. The kit teaches children about the properties of natural gas and other gases; how natural gas is formed, extracted from the environment, transported, and used; provides historical perspective and also deals with conservation of the resource. The kit contains a colorful storybook; master coloring sheets, which are used in the language arts and art activities; a portfolio which contains suggested teaching strategies and activities ranging from science to language arts.

Teachers interested in ordering additional **Mini Volts and Wastey Watts Storybooks** or **Natural Gas Storybooks** can do so. Each additional book retails for $3.25. Those teachers unable to obtain the "Mini Volts and Wastey Watts" kit or the "Natural Gas Storybook" kit because of lack of sponsorship in their area may order the kits directly from the National Energy Foundation for the following prices: "Mini Volts Wastey Watts" kit-$24.95; the "Natural Gas Storybook" kit-$4.75. Orders must be prepaid and include $2. or 10%, whichever is greater, to cover shipping and handling charges. To order the above materials or for more information on other materials provided by the National Energy Foundation, write to:

Director of Curriculum
National Energy Foundation
5160 Wiley Post Way, Suite 200
Salt Lake City, UT 84116

To determine if you are in a sponsored service area, you can write or call the following NEF directors:

Kay McEnulty-Armstrong
NEF Midwest Regional Director
408 West Campus
Wichita, KS 67217
(316) 522-3909

Diane Gratland
NEF Northwest Regional Director
22810 Woods Creek Road
Snohomish, WA 98290
(206) 568-4581

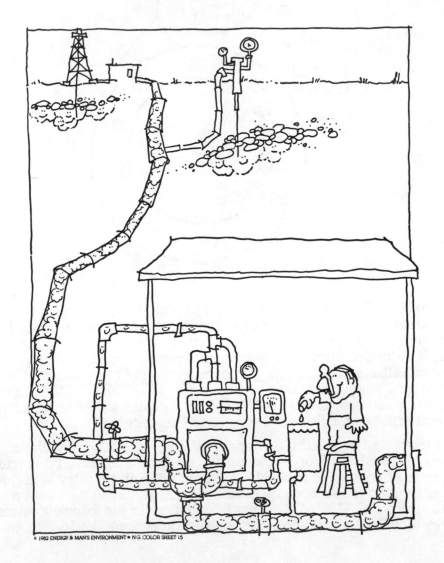

© 1982 ENERGY & MAN'S ENVIRONMENT • N.G. COLOR SHEET 15

Health

The Importance of Visual Development

One of the challenges you face as a teacher is following the rapid developmental changes of your students. An area of great importance is visual development. Homer Hendrickson (O.D., D.O.S.), president of the Optometric Extension Program Foundation, suggests as much as 80 percent of all learning occurs through the visual process.

The Optometric Foundation has a number of valuable pamphlets available. **Is Your Child Really Ready for School—Preschool Vision** points out that children's vision problems can be detected or prevented before affecting their success in school. It has been found that poor readers usually have healthy eyes, no muscle problems and 20/20 "perfect" sight, called acuity. However, they lack other important visual skills ignored by the Snellen Wall Chart Test. That test is a common vision screening which tells only if the child can clearly see letters 20 feet away.

Other important visual skills which are required before the child starts elementary school are: fixation, tracking, binocular vision, convergence, stereopsis (determining relative distances between objects), field of vision, form perception, and eye-hand coordination.

Guide and assist visual development

These abilities and skills are learned much better by the preschool age child when you know how to judge the child's progress and how to guide and assist this vision development. The **Preschool Vision Checklist** brochure has been created to provide enough information about vision development so you can make intelligent observations, and know when and where to help the child. The checklist, which accompanies these notes about vision, can be your way of knowing where on the scale the child is in developing the necessary visual abilities and may signal any potential visual problems.

Some clues to classroom visual problems are: unusual redness of eyes and lids; excessive tearing, rubs eyes during or after short periods of visual activity; squints or covers one eye; blinks excessively at nearpoint activities, not elsewhere.

The **Vision Hygiene** pamphlet gives basic guidelines for reducing visual stress, including proper lighting and posture.

By the time your pupils reach the age of 5, their eyes will become the guides and the monitors for all their actions. You can facilitate this development by proper guidance and providing the opportunities to practice visual skills which are essential for school readiness and all lifetime activities.

These three pamphlets are available for $1 with a business-sized, SASE, along with your request to:

Optometric Extension Program Foundation Inc.
2012 South Dimier Street
Santa Ana, CA 92705
(714) 250-8070

Teachers also need to observe the hearing development of their young students in the classroom, for children learn to talk by listening and practicing what they hear. Even mild hearing losses may result in children missing much of the speech and language around them.

"Don't Put Anything in Your Ears!"

This reminder, along with other helpful hearing tips, are included on a colorful poster—"Healthy Hearing," from the National Association for Speech and Hearing Action. Cartoon animal characters pass on these important pointers for safeguarding children's hearing, while a classroom activity guide supplies the teacher with questions and activities to help the children understand the poster and impress how valuable the sense of hearing is to learning.

One section of Healthy Hearing Poster.

Designed for classroom use, the packets contain 25 black and white posters to be colored by the children and taken home to share with parents. The poster is available for $2.25 and the packet, including one full-color poster, 25 black and white posters and classroom guide, is $5.25.

To order **Healthy Hearing Poster**, send remittance to:

> National Association for Hearing and Speech Action
> 10801 Rockville Pike
> Rockville, MD   20852

Teachers have a key role in helping children stay healthy. The American Heart Association has developed a program for preschool and kindergarten children, the **Heart Treasure Chest**, which is directed toward prevention steps dealing with diet, physical activity and habits related to the care of the heart.

Heart Treasure Chest

Lub-dub, lub-dub, lub-dub.

This sound which the children are making at the Small Faces Child Development Center (Seattle, WA) is the sound of a heartbeat. They have become aware that each of them has a heart about the size of their fist, and that it pumps blood all through their bodies via vessels.

The awareness of one's heart, how it works, how to tell if it's healthy, and how to care for it through proper diet, physical activity, and rest is the focus of **Heart Treasure Chest**, a program developed by the American Heart Association.

The Heart Treasure Chest is presented in three modules: 1) The Work of the Heart and Ways to Tell if It's Healthy, 2) Physical Activity and Rest, and 3) Heart-Healthy foods. Each includes the following information: Key concepts; background information for teachers; what 3- and 4-year olds and kindergarten children can understand; planning activities; and directions for activities.

Additional resources include reinforcement activities, adult resources, completion certificates and a description of "Heart Notes" newsletter for parents which is designed to "encourage parents to adapt their lifestyles to ensure healthier lives for themselves and their children."

The program provides many "hands-on" and sensory experiences for preschool children. These activities can be adjusted to present concepts at a more complex level for kindergarten children.

Sandi Jurick, a teacher at Small Faces Child Development Center, participated in the pilot program of Heart Treasure Chest and found the children were fascinated by the chart showing the position of the veins and arteries. "After looking at the chart," she explained, "they would lay on large sheets of paper, have their body outline traced and then use marking pens to show where the blood flowed in their bodies.

"An easy and quiet way to help children learn that active play makes their heart beat faster," adds Jurick, "is to have them jump on a small trampoline and have them listen to their heart beat."

Connect physical activities with heart awareness

Lynn Sherwood, American Heart Association representative in Washington, noted that if children participate in this type of experience, they often connect physical activities with heart awareness.

At the Little Church on the Prairie Child Care Center (Tacoma, WA), Linda Merritt, another program participant, noticed many children enjoyed the water play. It provided a "hands-on" demonstration of how the heart works.

"They would place their hands on a water-filled balloon and feel the pumping of the water as it flowed in and out with the aid of a baster. They also were fascinated watching the red-colored water flowing through the tubing," she continued, "illustrating how the blood vessels carry the blood."

The "doctor's corner" was a popular play area at both schools. The teachers borrowed a selection of materials from their local hospital, including stethoscopes, hats and gloves. "The children would spend hours using the stethoscopes, listening to the heart beat of their friends," Jurick said.

The **Heart Treasure Chest** includes:

For the teacher: Curriculum guide; **Heart and Blood Vessel** booklet; and **Learning About Our Hearts** filmstrip, cassette and script.

For the parents: Heart Notes and Certificates.

For the classroom: Heart Child Poster; Inside Your Heart Poster; My Pulse Card; Stethoscope Card; **Heart Songs, Grow Music and Heart Sounds** cassette; **Take Care of Your Heart** filmstrip and cassette; **Hear Your Heart** book; Healthy Heart Home Game; 16 Physical Activity and Rest Cards; Fruit and Dip Recipe Cards; Stethoscope; Syringe and Plastic Tubing.

Other Heart Treasure Chest promotional ideas and materials (stickers, balloons, posters, etc.) are also available separately.

To order, contact your local American Heart Association office or write to:

American Heart Association National Office
7320 Greenville Ave.
Dallas, TX   75231

Another method of preventing outbreaks of infections is through proper handwashing techniques. A national disease reduction campaign is sponsored by the Department of Health and Human Services, and implemented through the Scrubby Bear Foundation.

New Spokesbear Says "Scrub Up"

If all goes as planned, **Scrubby Bear**™may become as well known to young children as "Smokey the Bear."

This new mascot (originally T. Bear) is the "spokesbear" of a national "Handwashing Prevents Infection" campaign sponsored by the Scrubby Bear Foundation. Through the use of posters, stickers and other communication forms, the program stresses the importance of handwashing as the single most effective means available to prevent the spread of infection.*

Teaching children and staff the proper hand washing techniques is required, however, before this can be effective. "Scrubby Bear" says for best results:

Use SOAP and WARM RUNNING WATER
SCRUB your hands vigorously
WASH:
    Backs of hands
    Wrists
    Between fingers
    Under fingernails
RINSE well
DRY hands with a paper towel
Turn off the water using a PAPER TOWEL instead of bare hands

How do germs spread?

To help children understand more about how to prevent the spread of germs, Patrice Rawlins, R.N., M.N., and health services coordinator, has developed training sessions for children and teachers which she described in her article, "Training Children" in the **Texas Child Care Quarterly**, (Austin Texas Department of Human Services, Spring 1986). The children's session includes a discussion and three demonstrations:

In the discussion, adults and children talk about germs (What do germs do? What do they look like? How do germs spread?). They also discuss how to keep from spreading germs to friends (Wash your hands. Cover sneezes and coughs. Throw away dirty tissues. Keep your fingers out of your nose and mouth.)

The first demonstration requires a ball of yarn with a "germ," a round fuzzy creature with large, sticky feet, attached to one end. One child holds the ball of yarn while the "germ" is passed to each child. As a result, yarn is strung throughout the group.

The second demonstration requires a bowl of "pretend" germs, such as flour or powder. As the trainer or caregiver, you take a small handful of flour and pretend to sneeze, letting the "germs" fly. Show the children the "germs" on your hands. Touch your contaminated hands to your clothing. Touch a child's hand with your contaminated hand, and have the child touch another child.

In the third demonstration, show children how to wash their hands properly. Have children make special buttons to wear and posters to hand in to the center. Reinforce the hand washing discussion at least once a week.

A training staff education session can consist of a 20-minute discussion of the various ways germs can be spread, the incidence of ill children in child care, appropriate times for hand washing, and proper hand washing techniques. To demonstrate hand washing, use Glo-Germ, a special kind of fluorescent oil. Instruct the staff to rub Glo-Germ into their hands and then wash them. Shine a black light on their hands to show the residual Glo-Germ and the parts of the hands which were not cleansed thoroughly. *

Glo-Germ detects missed dirt

"**Glo-Germ** is also safe for children to use and is required in hand washing campaigns by school systems in Las Vegas, Fort Lauderdale and many other districts around the United States," said Joe Kingsley, President of Glo-Germ Co.

"School nurses are trained to set up programs so that all the children in the school system can learn the skill of proper hand washing," Kingsley said. "The Glo-Germ is rubbed on the children's hands and then the children are asked to wash their hands. When they return to the room and place their hands under a black light, invariably the light will show oil remaining between the fingers and the sides of their hands."

There are two packages available. One contains an 8-ounce bottle of Glo-Germ oil (which will cover approximately 35-45 pairs of hands), a 4-ounce container of Glo-Germ powder, and a battery-powered black light ($49.95). The other packet contains an 8-ounce bottle of oil and 4-ounce container of powder and an electric hand-held black light ($89.95).

* Reprinted by permission from "Training Children," **Texas Child Care Quarterly**, Vol.9, No.4.

Readers interested in obtaining a Glo-Germ package may note in their order that they read this article in **Early Educator's Tool Box** and Mr. Kingsley will give a 10 percent discount and replace the powder with a second bottle of oil (which is easier to administer). Additional bottles of oil are available for $14.95. For more information on Glo-Germ products or ordering call (800) 842-MOAB, or write:

Glo-Germ Co.
P.O. Box 537
Moab, UT 84532

*For more information on the "Scrubby Bear—Handwashing Prevents Infection" campaign, write to:

Scrubby Bear Foundation, Inc.
1155 15th St., N.W., Suite 500
Washington D.C. 20005

Every early childhood classroom has its fill of the cold and flu "bugs" that go around the community. Keep your eyes open, however, for those cold symptoms that don't disappear.

Tips for Teachers

No matter what the season, you can often find a child in the classroom who has a constant runny nose. Allergic disease is the most common illness in children, states the Asthma and Allergy Foundation of America. "Therefore, it is likely that you may have several allergic children in your class."

One way to help your students is to be alert to symptoms so parents can be consulted. **Tips for Teachers—The Allergic Child**, a pamphlet from the foundation gives information on hayfever, insect bites, food and skin allergies and asthma. It also includes a useful section which answers common questions concerning these allergic reactions.

Some suggestions given to help avoid allergic reactions in the classroom are:

1) Avoid having the allergic child sit near air vents which can be dusty or to participate in cleaning the blackboard.
2) Be aware that an allergic child may be sensitive to small pets kept in the room.
3) Note that the odor of some commonly used products such as glue, paint and detergents can cause allergic symptoms.

It is important to recognize, the authors explain, that allergies are not contagious and patience and skill may be needed to help the child through periods of tension. This guide is not intended as a substitute for instructions given by the child's doctor through the parent. However, it can help you become informed and improve the well-being of your students.

Tips for Teachers is available in bulk orders. For more information on this or other pamphlets available, write to:

Asthma and Allergy Foundation
1717 Massachusetts Avenue NW
Washington D.C. 20036

Safety

Behind a pile of large boxes stands a little girl. "Can any of you see her?" asks kindergarten teacher, Novella Miller. (Henry Heights School, Lake Charles, La.)

No, the class is not playing hide and seek, but participating in a demonstration to show that children can be hidden by large objects. This is one activity included in the National Safety Council's **Preschool Pedestrian Safety Program** which Ms. Miller has been using in her classroom.

"Streets are Not for Little Feet"

Every year from 450 to 600 children ages 3-5 are killed in pedestrian-traffic accidents, according to the Safety Council. The most common accident for this age group occurs when the child, usually on his own block, runs between parked cars into the roadway. To help prevent that situation there are lessons in the safety program based on the concept that cars are bigger than children (and can hide them) and that children should always stop at the curb, because it separates a safe area from a dangerous area.

The program reaches preschoolers as they first begin to experience traffic by using methods specifically geared to their abilities and limitations. Because many children are still learning to match sounds with objects and determining the meaning of those sounds there is a lesson on listening and learning the different sounds of traffic: cars, trucks, buses and motorcycles. It includes being able to tell if a car is coming closer by the fact that the sound is getting louder.

Repeat lessons throughout the year

Because many children have short attention spans and have difficulty in remembering sequential ordering, the program uses elementary vocabulary and presents ideas one at a time. "I spend two to three days on each lesson," Ms. Miller said, "and continually repeat them throughout the year—both in the classroom and when we are outside by a street."

The main objective of the **Preschool Pedestrian Safety Program** (written by Janice Sutkus and Illustrated by Janet LaSalle) is to teach preschoolers to stay out of the street when not with an adult. It is conveyed in four ways: streets are for cars; sidewalks are for walkers; automatically stop at the curb; and always cross the street with someone older. However, it also prepares them for later instruction by teaching them about motor vehicles and how walkers can stay safe.

The program also avoids presenting bad examples the child might mimic. The Safety Council has found that establishing a basis for development of safe habits brings best results because the habits are automatic and do not depend on reasoning ability or forethought.

At the beginning of each lesson is a list of vocabulary words. By drawing attention to the new words as they come, explaining their meaning and using them repeatedly in context, it helps children to grasp the lesson's message.

Life-saving lessons

"We found the parents have gained a lot from the program and have been able to reinforce the vocabulary and safety habits at home," Ms. Miller said. "This has been possible through the parent letters which remind them that their child is learning a life-saving lesson and that they can help by doing the follow-up activities at home."

Each lesson also includes large selections of "Discussions and Demonstrations," "Outdoor Activities," and "Classroom Activities." One graphic demonstration in Lesson 3: "Stop at the Curb" reinforces that fact the a curb is not a safe place to play—that a car that is stopping at the curb might make a mistake and ride over the curb. The teacher demonstrates this by rolling a ball down an imaginary street with blocks for curbs. Rolling the ball again, harder and faster, she can cause it bounce over the curb made of blocks. Pretending that the ball is a car, the children can see that as the ball rolls over the blocks, a car can also go over the curb.

Rhyming sheets for each lesson are very popular with the children, as is Watchful Willie, a plush Dakin dog, that teaches the children safety lessons through dialogue scripts.

"Willie, the program's mascot, is very special to the class," Ms. Miller said. "The children get very interested whenever he appears, as he did the other day when he came from behind the curtain with a traffic light to show them," she continued.

Correlate traffic program with other curriculum

"I also correlate the traffic program with other parts of the curriculum," Ms. Miller explained. "I use it in language arts to help with our left to right progression. After talking about traffic lights, I place a green light on the left hand column and a red light on the right hand column of the page. The children know to start with the green light and stop when they come to the red light," she said.

The program kit contains "Watchful Willie"; two-colored poster 17"x22" warning "Stop at the Curb!"; three-ring plastic binder which holds a reproducible letter of introduction to parents and five lessons. Each lesson contains a two-sided, reproducible coloring sheet with instructions to adults; four 17"x22" coloring posters, puppet dialogue script, illustrated rhyme, planned activities and vocabulary words. The kit is stored in a green, cardboard car which doubles as a colorful training aid for the children.

"We keep the posters up in the room to remind us of our safety lessons," Ms. Miller said. "The children have gotten a lot out of the program and when they reach a curb they know to 'Stop, Listen and Look Always'!"

The **Watchful Willie Preschool Pedestrian Program Kit** is available for $25. To order, obtain an order form by writing to:

> National Safety Council
> P.O. Box 11933
> Chicago, IL   60611

Learning by Doing

"Stop, listen, look left, then right, then left again, now cross," says 4-year-old John before he crosses the street to pick up the mail under the watchful eye of his teacher, Nadine Swanson. This special job is part of the reinforcement of traffic skills John has learned at Vermont Hills Preschool (Portland, OR).

Swanson teaches a traffic safety unit which focuses on the American Automobile Association's series of booklets, **Preschool Children in Traffic**.

The program has two primary objectives. The first is to prevent children from running into the street and the second is to help them develop habits necessary for safe performance in the traffic environment. Emphasis is placed on "Learning by Doing," and the repetition of "adult-directed" experiences.

As explained in the Parent's Guide, young children are unaware of traffic laws and how they, as individuals, fit into the traffic system. In addition to such developmental characteristics as short attention span, impulsiveness, and thinking that is typically based on impulsiveness, and thinking that is typically based on what they see rather than reason, there are physical developments that place them at a disadvantage.

Developing skills for eyes and ears

Their visual perspective is poor because of their height and the fact that young children are typically farsighted and side vision is not well developed. However, according to the program guide, they can begin to develop skills for using their eyes and ears to gather details concerning traffic if they are guided to do so.

Swanson begins the year by introducing Booklet 1, "When I Go Outside," (Ages 2½ to 6) which deals with helping the children learn to stay out of the street. They learn where to play and walk while outside and how to tell when a car is coming, going away or backing up. Each child is supplied with a book and they go through it together (with the help of an aide).

After reading the booklet which discusses drivers, walkers, curbs and streets, the class goes outside and looks at the curb, sidewalk and talks about car movement in the street. "Then I take them over to my car," Swanson explains, "where I start the motor and show them what the back up lights look like." She has found that all these type of experience help to reinforce topics discussed in the classroom.

At the end of the lesson, Swanson allows the children to take their books home. The parents, who have been informed of the traffic safety program and booklets, are asked to re-read the booklet and have it available for the child to refer to if needed.

Provide children with opportunities to practice

The second booklet, "I Listen and Look for Cars" (Ages 3 to 6) encourages children to assume some responsibility for their own actions on residential streets close to home while with adults. The introduction emphasizes the need for teaching each skill—stop, listen and scan in both directions separately and allowing the children time to practice on a straight section of a street before attempting to cross at an intersection. The booklet uses the terms "one way" and "the other way," but Swanson has found it worthwhile to have the children look back in the initial direction again to insure safety.

Booklet 3, "How I Cross the Street" (Ages 3-6), explains what intersections are and how to use them. In the parent's notes it suggests an excellent learning experience is to provide the children an opportunity to observe vehicular and pedestrian traffic from the second or third floor of a building, and thus learn more about the complex traffic situation at intersections.

The fourth booklet, "The Traffic Signal Light" (Ages 5 to 6), introduces traffic signs found on posts and those that hang over intersections. It emphasizes that walkers must still look for cars coming or turning even though the light is green and his signal says walk.

Along with this series, Swanson uses a variety of traffic safety activities. She culminates the initial program by allowing each child to cross the street alone in front of the school.

"This is quite a big step for the children," she explains. "After much preparation, we take the class and aides outside and down to the grass by the curb. An adult goes across the street and I stay with the child. Each student has a turn listening, looking and crossing the street. It's quite an involved activity, but a very important one for children this age."

To obtain the **Preschool Children in Traffic** series:

Contact your local American
Automobile Association Club
regarding the availability
of these materials.

The American Automobile Association has also designed a series of booklets to assist you in providing for the traffic safety education of children. Simple pictures about traffic form the basics for real-world child and adult experiences. By using the booklets you can help your students to assume pedestrian responsibilities progressively as their capabilities increase.

Preventing Big Spills on Big Wheels

"Someone help Berton! Stop!" shouted Chris.

Poor Berton! He was shaking all over. Big cars were zooming by. Horns honked as people tried to drive around Berton the Big Wheel. He wanted to get out of the street, but without Mark to push his pedals, he couldn't move.

Berton the Big Wheel, a unique character of the American Automobile Association's Traffic Safety Program alerts children to the importance of riding safely on Big Wheels or other riding toys. The eight-page booklet (**Berton the Big Wheel #3208**), with illustrations, is an exciting way to tell children to look for cars backing out of driveways—being aware of exhaust smoke and backup lights. It also stresses avoiding parking lots as play areas, driving with control and being a courteous driver on the sidewalk.

The American Automobile Association has other pedestrian and bike safety booklets and posters available for use in the classroom.

Traffic Safety Posters (#3021) In calendar form, these free posters designed by students present safe pedestrian and bicycle driving rules.

Parents, Children and Traffic (#3194) A pamphlet which relates how a young family taught their 3-year-old son to say out of the street. Geared for apartment and city living, it is an excellent resource for teachers and parents.

To obtain these materials:

Contact your local American Automobile Association Club regarding the availability of these materials.

Accidents involving fire, safety, and the ingestion of foreign objects and poisons affect young lungs and cause thousands of preventable deaths each year, according to Robert Simmons of the American Lung Association of Los Angeles County. In response to this problem, the Los Angeles Association has created the **Safe at Home** curriculum to teach young children safety skills, and to reach parents through the instruction of their children.

New Safety Program Well Received

The 4-year-olds sit quietly and listen intently to the sound of a smoke alarm and the crackling of a fire, as they turn the pages in their **Safety Siren** books. As part of Paivi Lane's preschool class at the YWCA in Pacheco (Calif.), they are participating in the new **Safe at Home** program developed by the American Lung Association of Los Angeles County. The 40-lesson program curriculum covers lung safety as well as water, ingestion and fire safety.

The **Safety Siren** book, which can be reproduced, along with the correlating sound track on a cassette tape, teaches children to recognize sounds and procedures that would assist them in case of a fire. It is one of many activities in the fire safety section. Other topics include identifying items that start fire; recognizing tools used by fire fighters; learning the Stop! Drop! and Roll! safety maneuver; and campfire safety.

Program designed for variety of learning styles

"Fire safety skills are so important to young children and I found this program which deals with prevention and emergency precautions very useful," Lane said. "The program has activities which are good to use with all our children. I particularly liked the **Safety Siren** book because even the 2- and 3-year-olds were able to pick up information from it and improve their auditory and recall skills," she said.

Melissa Mullins, teacher at the Mary Ann Frostig Center of Educational Therapy (Pasadena, CA) found she could easily adapt the materials to her developmentally disabled preschoolers. "The children learned a lot from the various activities because there was a great deal of visualization and tactile learning that took place," she said.

A unit on "Ingestion Safety" is unique to this program and is important to teach young children who are so susceptible to placing harmful items into their mouths. There is a wide selection of games which reinforce recognizing the difference between good food and drinks and those things that are poisonous or non-digestible.

Learning what is edible or inedible

Mary Moffet of the Le May Child Center (Van Nuys, CA) found her 4-year-old students were very receptive to all the activities. "The songs are excellent and the children can follow and play the games easily," she said. "In one particular game, the "Happy Face Game," the children decide what type of food is edible or inedible. They place cards into a can outfitted with a large smiling face. The "Happy Face" will eat only those foods that are good because they are cut specifically to fit."

Because this and many other activities in the program are self-correcting, they can be utilized in learning centers to reinforce the lessons taught.

"There are ingestion activities dealing with washing their hands before eating; the function of their front and back teeth; and the importance of chewing their food thoroughly," said Audrey Clark, Ph.D., co-author of the program.

"Stress the importance of sitting down while the children are eating," Clark said. "Children are much more likely to aspirate food while they are moving around. This often occurs when they are home eating snacks.

Learning how the lungs function, what happens when the breathing process is inhibited and why water must be kept out of the lungs, are topics covered in the lung safety unit.

The fourth unit on water safety teaches safety measures relating to hot liquid burns, swimming, boating, bathing and going out in wet weather. This unit is particularly applicable for summer, since it covers drowning prevention and the "Throw and Go" rescue strategy. This plan recommends that children should be taught to throw a flotation aid (if one is readily available) to the distressed person and then run for adult help—instead of jumping in the water to save another person.

Each activity lesson plan included in the **Safe at Home** book includes an objective, list of materials needed, method of presentation, follow up and teacher tips. The games to be constructed can be easily and inexpensively assembled according to simple-to-follow directions included. The black and white patterns are made to be reproduced by teachers. The audio cassette features five safety songs and the safety sounds that accompany the **Safety Sirens** talking book are included in the back pocket.

There is a strong parent component interwoven throughout the curriculum. An introductory letter, program summary, and home safety checklist precede the formal lesson plans. A home safety lesson to reinforce each set of new concepts introduced and to encourage active parent participation in the program, is included at the end of each module. The parent materials are also translated into Spanish.

"I was glad to be able to include the parents in the program by reproducing the parent letters, which include activities to review the concept of the lessons," Mullins said. "Our parents were very receptive and appreciated receiving a variety of home safety brochures which were supplied in the back of the program book," she said.

The **Safe at Home**—Early Childhood Safety Curriculum is available for $15, which includes shipping and handling.

To order, send remittance to:

American Lung Association of Los Angeles County
5858 Wilshire Blvd.
Los Angeles, CA   90036

Fire Message from Sesame Street

"Children under the age of five comprise 7 percent of the American population, but account for 17 percent of the fire deaths*," said Evelyn P. Davis, Vice President of Children's Television Workshop. A program developed to reduce this high vulnerability of 3-to-5-year-olds to fire and burns is CTW's **Sesame Street Fire Safety Program**.

Designed around the **Sesame Street** characters, Big Bird, Bert, Ernie and Oscar the Grouch who perform skits, and other activities including songs, fingerplays and games, the program entertains while reinforcing the fire safety messages appropriate for preschoolers.

Firemen seen as Darth Vadar

A prime example of how preschool children perceive happenings differently than adults is exhibited in the "Darth Vader" syndrome. The syndrome can be initiated by a child's inclination to run and hide if in danger, as in the case of a smoke filled room with a fireman in a large suit coming at him.

"This frightening sight of a big shape approaching with a face mask and breathing apparatus, is equated with a monster or Darth Vader," Davis said. "Allowing children to see firemen dressed in their 'turn out' suits, with which they fight fires in, and giving the children a chance to touch and become familiar with his equipment enables them to be better prepared to cope with the situation if it arose later," she said.

The four major topics covered in the fire program are understanding fire and burns, smoke detectors, firefighters and firefighting, and fire escape plans and fire drills. In addition, the resource book concentrates on aiding adults in informing preschoolers that: matches are for grownups; put a burn in cool water; stop, drop and roll, if your clothes start fire; and crawl under smoke.

Continual practice of safety rules is necessary

It is important for preschoolers to practice safety rules in order for the rules to become a natural reaction, Davis said. Two songs in the program that can be used in this manner are "Cool Water" and "Stop, Drop and Roll." The theme of "Cool Water," which emphasizes putting a burn in cool water right away, can be reinforced during the year by having the children sing it each time they cook.

"Stop, Drop and Roll", includes an exercise that teaches children the proper thing to do when their clothes start on fire. The authors of the **Fire Safety Resource Book** note that small children will need help doing the exercise before they can perform it themselves and continual practice will be necessary before children understand when to use this life-saving activity.

The **Fire Safety Resource Book** with record ("Cool Water" and "Stop, Drop and Roll") is available in English or Spanish for $2.50. Special bulk order rates are available on request.

Reinforcement of the themes of the fire program is available through the **Big Bird Fire Drill Book**. This 15-page book, though small(5 ½-inch X 6-inch), is well illustrated with colorful pictures depicting Big Bird learning the safety rules. It is available for $2.50.

To order **Fire Safety Resource Book** and **Big Bird Fire Drill Book**, send request and remittance to:

Children's Television Workshop
Dept. FS
One Lincoln Plaza
New York, NY 10023

*Findings quoted from "The Sesame Street Fire Safety Project," **Fire Safety Resource Book,** (Children's Television Workshop, 1982).

There are hidden hazards around the classroom that teachers should be aware of. Art supplies and playgrounds can contain materials which may cause an accident. The following resources can help you eliminate these from your school or center.

Art Supply Safety

How many times have you explained the proper use of art materials to your students, only to find a youngster licking paste-covered fingers?

Common art materials are often considered safe to use with children, but that is not always the case. Research conducted by the Center for Occupational Hazards in conjunction with the New York City Department of Health (Health Training Program), studied the types of art materials used in city day care and pre-school programs. There were 81 different art materials found in the ten surveyed schools. Of these, only 20 products could be considered safe.

How can you be sure the materials your students use are safe?

One way is to read **Children's Art Supplies Can Be Toxic**, an informative and useful eight page data sheet by Perri Peltz and Monona Rossol (Center for Occupational Hazards, 1984). They believe it is best to choose products whose labels clearly indicate what the product's ingredients are and how to contact the manufacturer. Even common materials such as some modeling compounds or paste contain wheat flour which may provoke an allergic reaction in particularly sensitive children.

Labels can be misleading

"Be cautious," they note, "of labels which state the product is 'non-toxic'. This law has many limitations but the most important is that it only identifies products which are 'acutely' toxic. This means that not only allergy-causing chemicals can be labeled 'non-toxic', but so can products which cause cancer, birth defects, and a host of chronic diseases. In addition, the tests are designed to identify acute hazards for adults, not children. (Note—In July 1986, a federal law was being drafted to ban these product from the elementary school.)

"The non-toxic label on art materials is misleading and lulls parents and teachers into a false sense of security," Rossol said.

An additional safety check is to look for an AP or CP seal of approval on the package. These seals certify that the Arts and Crafts Institute has found the art materials non-toxic to the body, even if ingested.

A product which may not be toxic, but is considered dangerous, is the scented felt tip marker. Because the markers emit a strong, fruit-like odor, the children associate them with food and may taste them. "This attitude and behavior toward art materials is especially dangerous because of children's great susceptibility to toxic materials." (**Art Hazards News**, Sept. 1984)

Children absorb toxic materials into their bodies more readily than adults because of their body development and more rapid metabolism. They are also at a higher risk because of smaller body weight: a toxic material is more concentrated in a child's body than in a larger adult. Because many materials are toxic through ingestion, it is recommended that shellacs, paint pigments and ceramic glazes be removed from programs which deal with young children.

Inhalation and skin contact are other routes through which toxins can harm children. The common occurrence of cuts and abrasions on hands increases the possibility for absorption. The authors emphasize, however, that "burns, irritations, ulcers and allergic dermatitis (rashes, etc.) can result from even brief contact with some art materials."

Type of program affects hazards

Do you teach day care, preschool or kindergarten children? The survey conducted by the Center and the New York City Department of Health, found that the type of school was very important in determining the types of hazards that exist:

> For instance, day care and preschool children who are enrolled in public programs that operate independently of a larger school system are exposed to fewer toxic materials than are children who share art facilities with a larger program and older children. (**Art Hazard News**, March 1984)

It was also noted that larger schools tend to have separate art facilities for use and storage of materials whereas children in smaller schools and day care programs often use the same room for arts and crafts and lunch.

Do you have handicapped children in your class? These children who are mainstreamed in the classroom are at a higher risk than the normal student. Peltz and Rossol stress that teachers must learn to plan programs which consider the illnesses, handicaps and physical limitations of these children. The "Art Supply Data Sheet" gives specific examples of the special care these children might require.

Show concern about the products you use

A source of further product safety information which may be available to teachers is the "Material Safety Data Sheet" (MSDS). This form, filled out by the manufacturer, provides a list of all ingredients for which there are health and fire standards, as well as other important facts. (Although manufacturers are not required by law to provide these forms to teachers and parents, reliable ones will send them.)

Peltz and Rossol feel that by requesting them you will show you are concerned about the products you are using, and that requesting MSDSs should be a routine part of a bid procedures for every product purchased by schools.

To receive a copy of **Children's Art Supplies Can Be Toxic**, a sample of **Art Hazard News** newsletter and a Center for Occupational Hazards publication list, send $1.60 and a SASE to:

> Center for Occupational Hazards
> 5 Beekman St.
> New York, NY 10038

Hidden Hazards on the Playground

Need to order some new sand for the sandbox outside? Steen Esbensen, author of **Hidden Hazards on Playgrounds for Young Children** gives this suggestion:

> The following procedure is recommended prior to accepting delivery of sand. Take a white cloth and place a sample of sand in the cloth to see if the damp sand stains or discolours the cloth. Discolouration or stain on the cloth indicates that the sand has not been sufficiently washed and that clay or dirt is still too prevalent for it to be used as effective sandbox sand.

We all want to provide safe, stimulating play opportunities for our children. With this guide you can systematically review the playspace in your school or child care center to determine if the equipment is well designed and constructed. If hazardous materials are found, it will direct you in ways to correct it.

Itemized details describing the design criteria for slides, climbing structures, swings, sand, surfacing and the total playground area are included.

It is a useful resource which Esbensen hopes will make playtime for your students safer and more stimulating in the future.

Esbensen is executive director of the Canadian Society of the Study of Education and ECE professor at the Universite du Quebec a Hull, Quebec, Canada.

To order **Hidden Hazards on Playgrounds for Young Children**, send $4 to:

> Steen B. Esbensen
> Universite du Quebec a Hull
> Case postale 1250, succursale "B"
> Hull, Quebec J8X 3X7
> Canada

There is nothing more upsetting than hearing the panicked words, "Have you seen my child?" Luckily not all missing children stay missing—instead they turn up at a friend's house or out walking with their dog. The following three resources approach various aspects of personal child safety: use of the telephone; the availability of a child locator card; and the teaching of wilderness survival.

Tele-Photo Phone Book

In the afternoon you receive a phone call from a distraught parent. "Is Tanya there?" Tanya, one of your five-year-old students, is missing from home and her father asks if you know her best friend's last name.

Often, when parents find their children are missing, they realize they do not know their child's playmates' full names or phone numbers.

Now there is a way to help those parents—supply them with a **Tele-Photo Phone Book**. This phone book, created by Nancy Lee of Pasadena, California, and developed by Mother Goose Distributing, includes a special section where photos and phone numbers of a child's best friends can be kept. It also provides space for parents to keep pertinent information regarding their families. In times of emergency, when children are missing, this material can save precious time.

The "Tele-Photo Phone Book" was created to allow even non-readers quick access to telephone numbers of people relevant to them: parents at work, family friends, police, emergency operators, etc. The book relies on identification of large color-in drawings of these people. Lee points out the children can color the uniforms to match those of local police and fire officials.

Children learn to identify "0" and "911"

The first section also deals with dialing basics to help train young children to recite their name, address and phone number, as well as identifying the "O" for operator and "911". A brief medical history that includes the child's age, height, weight, blood type, shots, medication, and fingerprints is included.

Lee said the book makes parents feel more secure if an emergency occurs when their children are home alone or when they realize their children are missing. However, it came in handy even when Linda Idoni of Los Angeles was at home. When her 2-year-old son, Brian, fell in the bathtub and smashed his front teeth, she froze in panic. Immediately Megan, his 5-year-old sister, went to the phone, picked up her "Tele-Photo Phone Book" and called the doctor.

The ability to use the phone book in an emergency situation is emphasized by Lee. She believes the book should be colored as a family project with adults explaining emergency procedures regarding the phone and how to use the phone book without fear.

At Martha Baldwin School in Alhambra, California, distribution of the "Tele-Photo Phone Book" was incorporated with a unit on safety. The teachers were supplied with many of the activity sheets included in an available teacher's kit.

Motivation was a vital part of the program, explained Donna Perez, Vice-Principal. "It was important to motivate the children to take the book home and complete it. Teachers let the children begin coloring the pictures at school and then spent time explaining how the phone numbers need to be filled in at home, how to use the book and the importance of finding a special place to keep it," she said.

"By coincidence, the children received their school pictures at the same time we were working with the 'Tele-Photo Phone Books'," continued Ms. Perez. "It worked out very well. The teachers helped attach a picture of the child on the 'This is my book' page and then recommended that they collect pictures of their friends which could be placed in their book at home."

Child Safety Night

A variety of methods were used to introduce the phone book to the parents. Announcements at the PTA meetings, information through newsletters and the use of the multilingual "Dear Parents" letter (from the teacher's kit) explained the use of the book and enlisted their support for completing the book. A "child safety night" was held for the parents where the agenda covered information on the "Tele-Photo Phone Book", child abuse and a variety of other topics.

The books are available individually for 55 cents apiece (up to 475), or as part of the "Teacher's Kit" for $20.00 plus $3 for postage and handling. (CA residents add 6.5 percent tax.) The Kit includes:

> Thirty paperback "Tele-Photo Phone Books"; 20 suggested activities (approximately half are geared toward the PreS-K student); Four reproducible worksheets; Two wall hangers; Two reproducible "cut-out" sheets for take home reminders; A "Dear Parents" letter explaining the use and enlisted of support; A reproducible "I did it right" certificate; A carrying bag.

In Erie County, New York, a bill has been introduced and passed to insure that all children throughout the county will be exposed to and receive the "Tele-Photo Phone Book." There are also school districts on the West Coast which distribute these books in cooperation with community-minded private companies.

For ordering or more information write request on letterhead and specify a street address, not a box number, and send to:

Mother Goose Distributing
512 Winston Ave.
Pasadena, CA   91107

Positive Action for Child Security

Picture taking is usually a prescheduled annual event. It is a service to supply parents with quality photographs of their child's early school days.

A factor recently being considered is that of safety. In numerous reports on missing children the key role of good, recent photos is emphasized.

One company now helping in an effort to have data available for parents whose children are missing is Portraits International Corporation. They have developed a child locator card, the **Protective Identification Composite** (PIC), which contains space for physical and medical information on each child. The 8X10 card has spaces for a wallet-sized photo and for fingerprints taken in the prescribed FBI manner. There are also front and rear full-length figures for placement of birthmarks, scars and other distinguishing features. An additional feature provided for parents is a detachable portion which contains "17 Vital Action Steps to Take If Your Child is Missing."

No obligation to purchase

The company provides PIC cards and an accompanying wallet-size color portrait FREE OF CHARGE for every child they photograph in the centers or schools they serve. They contract with the facility to photograph the children on a "speculative" basis. There is no obligation to purchase the product; yet they provide each parent with the protective aids as a public service—whether a portrait purchase is made or not. (Editor's note: Portraits International serves all states except Alaska and Hawaii; however, Nick Colquitt, Vice-President of Photography, emphasized that teachers from either of these two states who are interested in obtaining the PIC cards should contact the Portraits International main office at the number given below.)

Marietta Winters, director of a Kinder-Care Center in Mobile, Ala., has utilized the service and said she found it was very worthwhile. "Our parents were very receptive and supportive to the distribution of the PIC cards," she said. To help the parents complete the cards she arranged to have a representative from the local police department at the center to spend the morning fingerprinting the children. "This went very smoothly," she said.

A real working tool

The PIC card has been endorsed by the National Association of Child Care Management and approved by the Federal Bureau of Investigation. When developing this record for children, the card went through 11 of revisions before getting final FBI approval. Mike Ward, president of Portraits International, explained the reasons for their persistence:

> We wanted something that would be more than just a PR document. So we sought approval of our design from the FBI, with the idea that our card should be compatible with the FBI's computer tracing systems used in actual missing person situations. We wanted the card to be a real working tool if it was ever needed.

(**School Photography Industry**, Issue No. 1, 1985, Eastman Kodak Co.)

Any private or public institution interested in more information should call Portrait International's Customer Service Department at 1-800-633-2678 or write to:

Portraits International Corporation
1119 Dauphin Street
Mobile, Alabama 36604

Hug-A-Tree and Survive

One of the greatest fears a person of any age can experience is being alone and lost. **Hug-A-Tree and Survive** is a program aimed at teaching children to hug a tree once they know they are lost. The program directors explain that hugging a tree and even talking to it calms the child down and prevents panic. By staying in one place, the child is found far more quickly, and can't be injured in a fall.

The program was started in San Diego, California after a group searched for a 9-year-old boy who died in local mountains. The assembly program presented by search and rescue or law enforcement organizations, explains to children how not to get lost and how to be spotted and found. It is recommended for children 5 years and older but program developers have found that some 4-year-olds have seen the program and benefited from it.

This survival concept was proven successful when Elijah Fordham, 4, was rescued after being separated from his parents in the Sierra Nevada mountains. He remembered that he had been taught to talk to a tree if he got lost. Even though the temperatures dropped to the 40s after dark and he was without food or water, he was found by searchers 23 hours later still talking to his friend—a hollow tree trunk.

Children are familiarized with the types of people who will be looking for them. Some children are afraid of strangers or men in uniforms, and don't respond to yells. They have actually hidden from searchers they knew were looking for them.

The presenters also describe ways to aid searchers by finding a hugging tree near a small clearing if possible, as well as ways to protect themselves until rescued.

Originally the goal of the directors was to inform the children in the San Diego area, but as of January 1986 were approximately 1,643 presenters trained in 38 states and in countries around the world.

For more information on **Hug-A-Tree and Survive**, send a legal size SASE to:

> Jacqueline Heet
> National Office Hug-A-Tree and Survive
> 6465 Lance Way
> San Diego, CA   92120

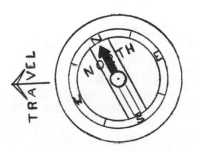

Multicultural Education

A class may be made up of children from various cultures or from a similar culture. In either case, each child brings to the group his or her own family beliefs, values, learning styles and traditions. To meet their needs it is essential for the teacher to understand and support each child as well as to develop positive relationships among members of the group.

A great deal has been written on cultural education and the development of self-esteem. Yet, how do teachers utilize this information to best promote multicultural concepts in the classroom?

The first step is for teachers to become aware of their own personal feelings about various cultures and their personal prejudices. Once this occurs, they can choose areas in which they will feel comfortable in teaching and thus become a positive model for cultural awareness—encouraging open communication in the classroom.

Culture and Children

The peak time for learning about ethnic identity seems to be between the ages of 3½ and 4½, according to Gayle Browne, Janet Howard and Mabel Pitts, authors of **Culture and Children**. The ways in which the child is like and unlike peers is increasingly important at this stage of their development and they should be given the opportunity to ask questions:

> Questions and comments about people's appearance start soon after the child is comfortable in speech, around 3 years. Questions often have to do with color of skin, hair or dress.

> Children quickly learn to judge whether their questions are appropriate. When questions are answered honestly, accurately, and in a way the child can understand, and if the non-verbal ones [responses] are positive, the child feels comfortable and accepted.

> Children feel "it's okay to ask questions, and it's okay to ask these sorts of questions." They learn that it is a good thing to be curious and excited about the world. They can focus on the answer if they sense that there is no hesitation or uneasiness in the adult.

Presents relationship between culture and child's personality development

Written in response to requests for ECE multicultural material in Texas, **Culture and Children** is a valuable resource designed to help integrate cultural experiences and concepts into any early childhood classroom. It presents the relationship between culture and the child's personality development—including the role of the family as a cultural unit. Six cultures are presented in depth for teachers interested in learning more about child-rearing, customs and languages of various ethnic groups.

"In children's programs, communication and appreciation of cultures should be as much a part of daily routines as hygiene or serving nutritious food," the authors notes. Multicultural education should also stress similarities as much as differences. Teachers should introduce ideas and information which are meaningful to young children and avoid overemphasizing exotic differences.

Building a memory bank of cultural experiences

This concept of stressing similarities is well developed in **Culture and Children,** which explores cultural classroom experiences in such diverse areas as aroma, games, festivals, language, literature, music and dramatics. They have found open communication of learning can involve the five senses so that children will build a memory bank of cultural experiences.

Making adobe bricks and building with them, using soups to teach about cultures and making kimonos and Masai necklaces are a few of the first-hand reports that describe how teachers have found and used tangible and inviting ways to help children experience culture.

Stressing the importance of being able and willing to understand other people's language and traditions is the focal point of the section on "Communication." Teachers can learn how others have taught their students Indian sign language and the Mexican Hat Dance, how to communicate with drums and how to play the "Blarney Stone" game, among other activities.

Highlighted throughout with illustrations and photographs, **Culture and Children** presents excellent examples of activities and provides directions for teachers to develop their own.

Culture and Children is available for $12. To order, send remittance to:

Texas Dept. of Human Services
Media Services Division 151-E
PO Box 2960
Austin, TX   78769

Introducing multicultural concepts into daily classroom practice is a method which helps to ensure that culture encompasses more than a special unit or holiday, according to Laverene Warner, author of "Learning Cultural Concepts through Daily Classroom Living,"(**Dimensions**, January 1985).

A common mistake made by teachers of young children is to plan a unit on the Mexican culture or on Indians, spending a week or two glorifying the culture with special projects, bulletin boards, books, and filmstrips. Of course, these units have merit, but the indirect message to children is that culture is like Christmas—it comes once a year and the remainder of the year is rather humdrum in comparison.

Multicultural materials that can be utilized throughout the year include storybooks, records and classroom manipulatives and games. The following articles describe where you can obtain these type of resources.

Create Games with a Native Flair

At the United Indians Preschool (Seattle, Wash.), Joy Ketah's Native American students play with unique educational toys: a buffalo wooden puzzle, lacing cards of Indian design, number cards illustrated with moccasins, tepees and Kachina dolls.

These and other games, including Lotto, wooden dominoes, and number readiness and matching puzzles, were created from patterns out of the **Daybreak Star Preschool Activities Book** (60 pages). The large-sized patterns (ranging from 5"X14" to 11"X14") allow for easy construction of the toys. After cutting and mounting the patterns on illustration board, they can be colored and laminated or covered by contact paper. Teachers can also find other uses for the patterns—such as displaying the number cards which measure 7"X10½" on bulletin boards.

Extend cultural involvement

These materials, published by the United Indians of All Tribes Foundation, were designed to provide children an opportunity to develop a positive self-image by learning skills from materials reflecting their own culture. "They are excellent hands-on activities that extend cultural involvement much better than simply making headbands and feathers," said Sharon Patacsil, co-author of the activity book and member of the staff at United Indians Preschool. "Our students are from a variety of tribes and are encouraged to identify with the art forms from the various sectional groups represented in the games. At the same time, a preschool that provides these kinds of materials to the non-Indian child builds an awareness and sensitivity toward a culture that is different from her/his own. It is hoped that a teacher using these activities can continue to introduce other facets of Native Americans throughout the year," she said.

Each game or activity is introduced with a description of the Native American art forms used—explaining their origin and meaning as well as suggested colors. The materials needed and the procedure for creating the games are also included. High school or college students working in the classroom are often excellent game makers, Ms. Patacsil said. "The students from Evergreen College who worked in our preschool helped a great deal in constructing the games which we use."

The **Daybreak Star Preschool Activities Book** is available for $5.75. Payment must accompany orders of less than $25. Make checks payable to Daybreak Star Press. Prices subject to change without notice. United States orders: add 15 percent for shipping and handling. Canadian orders: add 30 percent for shipping and handling, U.S. funds ONLY.

For further information or ordering, write to:

Daybreak Star Press
P.O. Box C-99305
Seattle, WA 98199
(206) 285-4425

Indian Legends Enhance Prereading Skills

"Long ago the traditional way for Yakima Indian children to learn was from exceptionally close association with family members, through constant observation and the ability to listen as oral lessons were repeated by grandparents or other elders. The old way of learning doesn't exist for many children today. Grandparents cannot compete with television," reports Violet Rau, publisher of Indian cross-cultural materials.

In response to this changing learning experience, Rau has compiled ten sets of **Literature from Indian Country** for young children which expand the use of oral storytelling.

"The legends use two beauties and strengths of the Indian cultures: memory (the ability to recall) and eloquence (the art of self-expression) to teach pre-reading skills," she said. "Children hear the legend first, then sequence the event of the legend with the illustrations. When the children know the legend, they use the hand puppets to retell the legend."

All the legends give an explanation of a natural occurrence. For example, the legend, "Bear and Ant Dance Contest," gives an explanation of why we have both day and night. The "Jackrabbit's Hunting Trip," tells why the jackrabbit has a brown spot on its bottom.

Each legend kit contain reproducible, sequenced pictures (8½"X11") and puppet patterns. The puppet patterns can be pressed onto pellon, a lining material that does not fray, and then colored with crayons and pressed. With puppets in hand, children love re-telling these simple Indian legends, in their own words, to one another.

The following legends are available:

"Foolish Frog" (#29-$3), "Turtles' Seeds" (#30-$5), "Coyote and Deer" (#31-$5), "Porcupine and Beaver" (#32-$3.50), "Jackrabbit's Hunting Trip" (#33-$4.25), "Curious Rabbit" (#34-$5), "Pheasant and Crow (#35-$3.50), "Snakes" (#36-$3.50), "Bear and Ant Dance Contest" (#37-$3.50), and "Giant Beaver Fight" (#38-$3.50).

Visiting Native American celebrations

Other material available are **Little Bears** and **Baby Bears Go Visiting** coloring book series. In each book there are 16 different detailed illustrations (8½"X11") showing the bears visiting a different region in North America where Native Americans gathered for celebrations. There are also 16 small (3¼"X3¾") identical cards which can be used for matching games. The pictures depict "Little Bear" dressed in authentic regional costumes and "Baby Bear" in Indian cradle boards. Discussion pages are included which describe materials that make up the clothing worn and a list of vocabulary and cultural activities. The coloring books are priced at $2 each.

The "Little Bear" series includes: #1-"Columbia River Plateau-Yakima", #2-"Columbia River Plateau," #3-"Pacific Northwest Coast," #4-"Plains," #5-"Southwest," #6-"Plains," (different from #4), #7-"Great Basin," #8-"Southeast," #9-"Woodland," #10-"California," #11-"Arctic Circle," #12-"Oregon".

The **Baby Bears Go Visiting** series includes: #1-"Plains," #2-"Southwest and Great Basin," #3-"Pacific Northwest Coast, Arctic Circle and Woodland," #4- "Columbia River Plateau and California", #5-"North American".

Walking in two worlds

Another interesting set of books is "Walking in Two Worlds" paper doll books ($2.50 each). They present two Native American children, Dawn and Red Eagle, with 24 changes of clothing which illustrate the two lives led my many American Indian children. One is the largely non-Indian world of community and school and the other is the traditional world at home. Having the paper dolls available for the 5-year-olds and making them into a felt board activity for younger students is another way to broaden their education and understanding of Native American culture.

A 52-page catalog which contains Indian kits, books and patterns is available for $2.50.

To order material, send item number and description. Shipping charges for orders totaling up to $6 add $1; $7 to $12 add $1.50; $13 to $20 add $2; $21 to $39 add $3; $40 to $100 add $4; more than $100, add 5 percent. Send order and remittance to:

Celia Totus Enterprises, Inc.
P.O. Box 539
Toppenish, WA 98948

Japanese Fairy Tales Enrich Storytime

The Monkey and the Cat, The Old Man who Made the Trees Bloom, and The Adventures of the One Inch Boy. What do all these stories have in common? They are all beautifully illustrated fairy tales from Japan.

The distributor of these books is JACP, the Japanese American Curriculum Project, which is located in San Mateo (CA). JACP stocks a large variety of Asian American curriculum materials for all age levels. The selection of resources for young children includes books such as **Ichi, Ni, San**, a primary level book to learn the numbers 1-10 in Japanese, as well as an assortment of Asian American dolls.

A 27-page catalog is available for $2. To order, send remittance and request to:

JACP, Inc.
414 East Third Ave.
San Mateo, CA 94401

Cultural Caravan Supplies Goods

Looking for multicultural materials to use in your classroom?

A store specializing in multicultural and multilingual resources is **Claudia's Caravan**, located in Alameda, California. Introducing multicultural ideas and information which is meaningful is the goal of owner, Claudia Schwalm.

A former teacher, she created the store so that educators would have a wide selection of multicultural materials to choose from. "Children need to be exposed to and learn to respect all cultures," Schwalm said. All items she stocks are evaluated for their accuracy and positive imagery.

Over 200 resources available

A catalog is available that contains over 200 entries including: resource and activity books, games and manipulatives, records, puppets and dolls. Some examples of the variety of cultural materials are:

Kwanzaa Coloring Book—illustrating the seven principles of the Black American holiday Kwanzaa with large simple drawings.

Gung Hay Fat Choy—a story of the Chinese New Year, told with color photos and simple text.

Grandfather's Stories-Vietnam—containing folktales and traditional values of the Vietnamese culture.

Spanish Alphabet Cards—ready for use as flash cards or bulletin boards.

Hanukkah—Full color photographs compliment this story of Hanukkah for children ages 4-12.

Inflatible World Globe—illustrates the world in full color, and comes with a stand.

To order a catalog, enclose $1 (refunded in first order) and send to:

Claudia's Caravan
P.O. Box 1582
Alameda, CA 94501

Special Needs

Advantages of Multiphasic Screening

The new year has begun and the children are settling into the routine, yet there are a few students who seem to be experiencing problems.

At the table, Kate, 4, is having difficulty using her scissors to cut out a piece of paper. She has also become frustrated while trying to string beads.

John, 3, wanders off during story time and is always asking, "What did you say?"

Luke, 4, avoids group games out of doors because he has difficulty in jumping and in throwing a ball.

These children may be experiencing a developmental delay. One way to help detect this is to recommend the child attend a Multiphasic Screening Clinic. Screenings are often performed by private or public health agencies such as county health departments. They may include: developmental tests, (personal-social skills, communication skills, fine and gross motor skills); vision and hearing tests; dental checkup; physical exam; and nutrition counseling.

The screening, which can pick up significant developmental deviations often overlooked in a physical checkup, is not a diagnosis but an initial process to identify children in need of more extensive evaluation. Screenings are not used to label children but to alert parents and teachers to a need for extra attention and help.*

It is important to remember that most developmental skills have a wide performance-age range. One child may master using scissors at the age of 2 and another at the age of 3—both are developing normally.

Because all children develop at a different rate it is important that the child is not stigmatized because of his/her lack of skills. However, it is vital to become aware of any problems which may exist, explains Carol Lloyd, author of an ERIC Clearinghouse **Fact Sheet** on Handicapped and Gifted Children.

Some areas in which a child may have learning difficulties are: Auditory Perception, Visual Perception, Distractability, Sequential Memory, Dyslexia, Motor Coordination, and Directionality.

If a child does have a learning problem or disability which goes undetected, that child's self-esteem may be undermined. Barbara Scheiber explains in **I Can Jump A Rainbow** (Foundation for Children with Learning Disabilities), "Learning doesn't apply only to the 3 Rs. It applies to all the things we absorb through our perceptions of our environment from early childhood on—from choosing clothes to wear, to playing games and making friends. Learning disabilities can affect every aspect of life."

Increase a child's success in school

By detecting a delay in development at the preschool level it may be possible to help children overcome potential learning problems before they start first grade. The Early Education Program of the Ferguson-Florissant School District supports this view. Their objective is "to effectively increase every child's chance for success in school—with particular concern for the young child with environmental deficiencies, developmental lags, and real or potential learning problems."

They screen all 3-year-olds. Those who indicate a possible learning problem or developmental lag are visited weekly at home by a specialist certified in Early Childhood Special Education. There is also a voluntary home and school program for all 4-year-olds that include testing, half-day school on Saturdays and other activities as well as home teaching visits.

Some useful materials this program has available are:

Screening and Diagnostic Procedures for Preschool Education (#50-$1.50)

Why Test for Parents? (#36-.50¢) Explains the importance of screening to parents.

Testing Program for Threes and Fours (#42-$3.50) Their testing and evaluation procedures, including a list of all instruments used. Plus a separate folder of district-developed screening and evaluation forms.

Providing for the PreSchool Child with Problems (Revised 1986, #41-$5) A description of testing and special services to 3- and 4-year-old children with problems; includes evaluation results.

Materials ordered from the Early Education Department which total less than $25 must be prepaid. Add $4 for shipping and handling for orders $12 and under. To receive more information on ordering large quantities, write to:

Early Education Program
Ferguson-Florissant School District
1005 Waterford Drive
Florissant, MO   63033
(314) 831-8809

The Foundation for Children with Learning Disabilities, a national institution devoted to public awareness of learning disabilities offers two resource publications: **Their World** ($4), an annual publication with stories about families who have coped with learning disabilities, and **FCLD Learning Disabilities Resource Guide** ($10), which features state-by-state listings of schools, colleges and diagnostic centers.

To receive these publications, send a check or money order to:

> FCLD
> Box 2929
> Grand Central Station
> New York, NY   10163

*I Can Jump a Rainbow, by Barbara Scheiber

If you find some of your students have potential learning problems or special needs, there are resources available which can help you accommodate them.

Meet Special Needs

"All children have special needs some of the time. Some children have special needs all of the time," writes Penny Deiner in **Resources for Teaching Young Children with Special Needs** (Harcourt Brace Jovanovich, 1983). This extensive (564 page), yet practical book, can help you become aware of and meet special needs of students within normal classroom routine.

A "special needs" child, explains Ms. Deiner, is one who requires adjustments in their curriculum or classroom. In the scope of her book this may include a child with a temporary need caused by a broken leg, one with newly divorced parents, a gifted youngster or a child with a long-term physical disability.

Changing roles of the teacher

The text is divided into two parts. The first part focuses on changing roles of teachers and gives information on necessary skills and how to develop them. The skills include working with parents and specialists, writing and implementing individualized education programs as well as teaching children with special needs in the regular classroom.

For teachers who need to focus on a particular special needs type of program, there are individual chapters dealing with the following needs: speech and language, hearing, visual, learning, physical, health, adjustment, culturally distinct, gifted and talented, and intellectual.

Ms. Deiner has successfully translated theory into practice and has intentionally used non-technical terms. The terms which may need to be known when talking to a specialist, however, are defined in a glossary.

The second part offers more than 300 activities designed to help children gain needed skills assessed in Part I. They are grouped into chapters by curriculum and are indexed in a variety of ways to make them easily accessible for a teacher with specific goals in mind.

Throughout the book, Ms. Deiner acknowledges the fact that teachers have the strengths and the needs of all children in their class to consider. She describes how specific activities can fit the total preschool/kindergarten program and ways to change activities to accommodate students with special needs. The key, she explains, is: "...you must find activities that give extra to special needs children, but are appropriate and enriching to all." The book was created especially to fill that role.

Resources for Teaching Young Children with Special Needs is available for $21.95, plus $2 for shipping and handling. (California residents—$1.50 shipping and handling and 6 percent tax.) To order send remittance and title of publication to:

> HBJ Book Store
> 1255 5th Ave.
> San Diego, CA 92101

Handicapped children's needs—same as all children

Anticipating new situations is a skill many early childhood educators have acquired over the years while dealing with young children. One of these situations—mainstreaming disabled children—is becoming more prevalent in the early childhood classroom setting; and teachers are finding they need to become aware of their attitudes and school policy concerning acceptance of a disabled child.

A teacher with no training or personal experience in working with a disabled child may be uncertain of her capabilities to teach the child effectively, provide a proper physical environment, or be able to cope with the additional stress and responsibility.

It is important at this point for the teacher to realize the skills handicapped children need are the same as those needed by all children. The classroom which offers social and play experiences and stimulating activities in a developmental setting is ideal for special children. This is the environment desired by those who stress mainstreaming—a place where a disabled child can come and be a part of a "normal" classroom with a minimum of modifications.

A common concern of teachers and parents of nondisabled children is that a teacher's time will be impaired with the added responsibility of teaching a disabled child. Teachers can gain knowledge about disabilities and alternative learning strategies as well as get support in making the best educational decisions by contacting specialists in the community.

Another valuable source of information, suggests Sandy Dietzen, handicapped coordinator at the Stockton (CA) Head Start Child Development Council, is a series of pamphlets, **Mainstreaming Preschoolers**, available from the U.S. Government Printing Office. Each book gives an introduction to mainstreaming and supplies specific information on a particular disability. The fact that mainstreaming can also be an especially valuable method for discovering undiagnosed handicaps, is also pointed out:

> A preschool teacher has the opportunity to observe and compare many children of the same age, which makes it easier to spot problems that may signal a handicap. Preschool may therefore be the first chance for some children to receive the services they need.

Mainstreaming Preschoolers

Mainstreaming Preschoolers has been developed by the U.S. Department of Health and Human Services. The books were written for teachers and others who work directly with handicapped preschoolers. The teaching techniques and activities included, however, are designed to help enhance skills in all areas of development and can be used with all preschool children—nonhandicapped as well as handicapped.

Guidelines for planning, teaching and preparing the physical setting are supplemented by valuable chapters such as "Parents and Teachers as Partners" and "Where to Find Help in Your Area."

These valuable resource guides are well organized and easy to read. They contain a great deal of practical information, each dealing with a particular disability. The **Mainstreaming Preschoolers** series includes:

> **Children with Orthopedic Handicaps** (S/N 017-092-00034-1) ($6.50)
> **Children with Health Impairments** (S/N 017-092-00031-6) ($6.50)
> **Children with Speech and Language Impairments** (S/N 017-092-00033-2) ($6.50)
> **Children with Emotional Disturbance** (S/N 017-092-00036-7) ($6.50)
> **Children with Visual Handicaps** (S/N 017-092-00030-8) ($6)
> **Children with Learning Disabilities** (S/N 017-092-00035-9) ($6.50)
> **Children with Mental Retardation** (S/N 017-092-00029-4) ($6.50)
> **Children with Hearing Impairments** (S/N 017-092-00032-4) ($6.50)

Orders must be accompanied by a check or money order made payable to the Superintendent of Documents, and include titles and stock number.

To order, send remittance to:

> Superintendent of Documents
> U.S. Government Printing Office
> Washington, D.C.   20402

"Handi-Box" for Special Help

"In order for teachers and aides to do a good job, they need to have a variety of materials to work with," said Bonnie Hollingsworth, education coordinator of the Warren County Head Start in Monmouth, Illinois.

A resource she has found useful for her teachers is the **Handi-Box**, a developmental curriculum designed for teachers in mainstreaming settings. The **Handi-Box** is suitable for handicapped and non-handicapped and was developed by Nancy Nordyke and the Jackson County Head Start (OR).

The curriculum provides approximately 375 objectives for developmental ages 2 through 5. The objectives, numbered and located individually on 5"x8" cards, are divided and color coded into six major curriculum areas: Gross Motor, Fine Motor, Language, Cognitive, Self-Help, Play and Socio-Emotional. Three of the curriculum areas (Cognitive, Language and Self-Help) are further divided into "Strands." For example, Language is divided into the categories of: Expressive, Receptive, and Reading Readiness.

"The **Handi-Box** helps teachers a lot by having references to draw from," Hollingsworth notes. "Each curriculum card includes procedures and activity ideas for individual, small or large group situations." If a 5-year-old is having trouble drawing a triangle, there are a number of objectives to follow. 1) Before having the child try to draw a triangle, see if he is able to draw a cross from a model (Fine Motor-22); 2) Have the child imitate drawing a triangle—initially it may be necessary to have a child imitate each stroke (Fine Motor-44); 3) Draw a triangle from a model (Fine Motor-45). Many objective cards also state related objectives to extend the skill learned.

"Because the objectives are divided by curriculum areas, it simplifies the procedure of locating the appropriate activity for the child or children," Hollingsworth notes. "The less time spent on research, the more time can be spent with the children."

The **Handi-Box** is available for $16 plus $2.50 postage and handling. To order send request and remittance to:

Jackson County Head Start
343 N. Ivy Street
Medford, OR 97501
(503) 779-5876

Stuttering—Prevention and Detection

As you observe your students experiencing new situations and sharing their discoveries, you'll notice some have difficulty with their newly gained communication skills.

Between the ages of two and five, practically all children exhibit speech disruptions. Although up to 80 percent of all children who stutter eventually develop normal speech without therapy, Audrey Isack and C.W. Starkweather of the Stuttering Prevention Clinic (Temple University) feel it cannot be overemphasized that to delay seeking help for the remaining 20 percent may mean the development of a well-habituated stuttering problem.

How do you know if a child is at risk for developing a stuttering problem? The answer is not always clear-cut. Speech specialists have divergent views on how stuttering can be diagnosed. Some feel nonfluency is a stage in normal behavior and will appear and disappear like other stages if left alone—whereas if the child is scrutinized, more fragmentation might occur.

Observe the child's fluency skill

Isack and Starkweather agree that some nonstuttering children show as many or more part-word repetitions as stutterers of the same age, however, it is important to observe the child's fluency skill (1) in a variety of environments (i.e. circle time, free play), (2) over a period of time, and (3) with a variety of listeners (i.e.: parent, peer, group of peers, and teacher)—and be prepared to detect a problem. Another sign to watch for, they add, is extreme reticence to talk. It is easy to assume that a child is not stuttering when he or she is not talking.

An important point to remember during this time of observation, is when communicating with a nonfluent child (with normal or abnormal disfluency) to respond to what he is saying, rather than how he says it. If you show worry or concern, the child will sense this and become hesitant or fearful. Kathleen Conover, speech and language pathologist, recommends when the child is talking and becomes nonfluent you should:

1) Maintain eye contact
2) Express no concern with your facial expression or posture
3) Listen to what he is saying and not how he is talking
4) Respond to what he says when he completes his sentence or question
5) Never tell the child to "Stop. Take a deep breath and start over" (This only indicates to your child that you are not pleased with the way he is talking.)

Remember, she continues, to provide an unhurried and calm speech model for the child to copy.

Isack and Starkweather suggest referring a child for further assessment if they show evidence of the following:

1) Long, as well as frequent, repetitions of words or syllables
2) Irregular rhythm of repetitions
3) Prolongs sounds
4) Pitch rises during production of vowels
5) Shows signs of tension, struggle or avoids talking
6) Intruded schwa (ə) (saying bəbəbaseball rather than bababaseball)

If you have difficulty locating a speech pathologist, the American Speech and Hearing Association will provide a list of services available by geographic area. In Washington D.C. area, call 301-897-5700. The toll free number is 800-638-TALK (8255).

"Because it is difficult to distinguish between normal non-fluencies and stuttering in young children, you must first be aware of normal fluency development," said Sheryl Ridener Gottwald, Peggy Goldback and Isack in their article, "Stuttering—Prevention and Detection," (**Young Children**, November 1985). This informative article identifies: symptoms of potential risk for stuttering; suggests ways teachers can enhance fluency in the classroom; offers sources for referrals as well as describes normal fluency development. Copies can be made to share with teachers if you receive the journal, or you can order a single copy of the article for $2 from:

NAEYC
1834 Connecticut Ave. N.W.
Washington D.C.   20009

Help for Hearing Impaired

An excellent resource for families with hearing-impaired children is the John Tracy Clinic, located in Los Angeles, California. Sandy Meyer, Director of Correspondence Education at this educational center for deaf and hard-of-hearing children, explained that the clinic's main goals are to encourage, guide and train parents to help their children through onsite services and its worldwide Correspondence Courses.

There are Correspondence courses available for deaf babies birth to 2 and deaf-blind children as well as a Preschool Correspondence Course. The **Preschool Correspondence Course** is directed toward parents of children 2 to 6 years old and consists of 12 lessons for home study, which includes information on: parent attitudes, communication, physical, emotional and social development and growth of children and activities to help deaf and hard-of-hearing children in their language and speech development. This course is free of charge to parents enrolled in the program and is available in English or Spanish.

The material included is very readable and well-organized, with each section color coded. The games included have variations for children at the beginning stages of language development as well as different levels of physical readiness. As the child develops, he can try some of the more advanced games and activities.

To enroll in the **Preschool Correspondence Course**, parents simply write to Sandy Meyer, Director of Correspondence Education and give the child's name and age, the family's full name and address, including the zip code.

Clinicians will adapt lessons

Once the child is enrolled, the clinicians will adapt the lessons based on what the parents tell them about their child's ability to understand conversation and to express himself in speech. "The clinicians will give suggestions about activities and learning games suited to where the child is now in language and speech," Ms. Meyers said.

After each of the 12 lessons, parents are requested to send in a report to the clinic commenting on how the lesson went and asking any questions. Once these are returned to the clinic, the next lesson is sent. It is an excellent resource for parents in need of support in their role of raising a child with a hearing disability.

Bound copies of the Correspondence Courses are available to teachers for a fee.

For more information write to:

John Tracy Clinic
806 West Adams Blvd.
Los Angeles, CA   90007

Children who participate in mainstreaming benefit from their contact with the teacher and the materials in the classroom. The most important aspect, however, is peer interaction and the relationships that develop.

Positive social interaction does not always occur spontaneously. It is the teacher's role to develop opportunities for positive experiences; yet, in order to accomplish this, the teacher needs to be aware of the differences in how children view disabled peers.

Remembering that young children experience the world in concrete, rather than abstract terms is important, according to Ms. Shelly Heekin, project coordinator of the **New Friends** program. This program deals with creating classroom environments and experiences to help young children understand and accept individual differences. She suggests using very concrete explanations or personal experiences when working with young children.

New Friends

You've been told that Molly, a child with a hearing disability, will join your class next week. Your first thoughts might deal with her need for special attention, her ability to communicate and concern about how she'll get along with the others.

But what about your students? How can you help them learn to understand Molly and to be comfortable relating to her and to other disabled persons?

One unique way to promote acceptance of others is to introduce **New Friends**, life-size, handmade dolls with various handicaps. They are part of the **New Friends Program** teaching that handicapped and normal children are more alike than they are different.

These sturdy, lovable dolls take on a personality. For instance, Hilda, portrays a capable 5-year-old whose favorite book is "Green Eggs and Ham," who has a pony named Jumper, who likes to swim, and who happens to have a hearing disability. Manuel tells children first about his kite flying and then about his artificial leg. And there are others. Children learn, through narration by the teacher, about their "New Friends" strengths and become aware of their differences in a positive way.

Caroline Mussellwhite has used the dolls successfully in a variety of learning situations. She is a speech-language pathologist at the Irene Wortham Center in Asheville, North Carolina, a small developmental day care center for children with cognitive and physical disorders. On one occasion she found that a child with cerebral palsy was planning to attend a local Sunday School class and offered to bring over Randy, a "New Friend," for a visit.

"When Randy arrived the children were fascinated listening to his jokes and some got involved sharing their own jokes with the class," Mussellwhite said. "Randy mentioned casually, how even though he couldn't walk, he was very excited about his new switches which enabled him to play with his battery-powered toys. The children had an opportunity to play with Randy, ask him questions and express their anxieties concerning his disability."

When it was time for Randy to leave he told the class that maybe next week he could bring a couple of his toys and switches to share. But then he exclaimed, "Oh dear, I can't come next week, but my friend Luke can. He can show you how neat they work."

"The class was shown a picture of Luke and learned of his interests, abilities and disabilities. After this introduction the children looked forward to meeting Luke and playing with him," Mussellwhite said.

The "New Friends Program" was developed by the Chapel Hill Training Outreach Project (North Carolina) when it was realized that disabled students were not the only persons affected by mainstreaming. Shelly Heekin, coordinator of the doll program, feels it's important for young children to understand and to be comfortable with people who have disabilities and to dispel common myths and stereotypes. She feels it's not fair to expect a positive response from a young child who is put in a new situation with different people. If they are fearful they may interact less and possibly tease or reject the disabled students.

Because preschool children's attitudes are flexible and their values are still forming, this is an excellent time to introduce disabilities in a positive manner.

The "New Friends" allow the children to satisfy their curiosity and to play out fears associated with handicapped conditions. "Boys and girls are encouraged to express their honest feelings when they meet new friends," Heekin explains. "In the end, they learn that it's all right to be different."

Guidelines for answering questions

The "New Friends Program" consists of a 155-page teacher's manual with seven units, available for $12. The first unit, "Preparing for Our New Friends," emphasizes self-awareness and encourages children to discuss similarities and differences among people. Succeeding units introduce the dolls and disabling conditions under the following headings: How We See: Meeting Vera; How We Hear: Meeting Hilda; How We Move: Meeting Manuel; How We Communicate: Meeting Camilla; How We Learn: Meeting Larry; Emotions and How We Feel: Meeting Freddie.

Each unit includes suggestions for introducing the various doll with sample scripts. The fully-developed scripts are meant as examples and the teachers are encouraged to tailor the dolls' dialogue to fit the program's goal—meeting the needs of their children. Trish Mengel, co-originator of the program suggests you can also involve the disabled child and parent with presenting the doll. The parent may also offer special information which would be useful.

In each unit there is also a discussion guide on specific disabilities, guidelines for answering frequently asked questions, class activities and resources. These include information on obtaining special equipment and appliances that can be used to provide "hands-on" experience for children. One exercise requires the children to try to put pegs in a pegboard while wearing smeared glasses to simulate a sight handicap. A copy of the basic doll pattern is also included.

Additional chapters contain activities to include families. By allowing the dolls to be available in the classroom throughout the year, it's possible for each child in the class to take a doll home for a visit.

There is also a "New Friends Family Album" packet available separately for $3. It is designed for the teacher and can be used to reinforce the concepts presented in the "New Friends" curriculum. The children create a chapter about themselves and then make new chapters as they meet "New Friends" during the year. The packet includes illustrations of "New Friend" dolls with proportionately scaled accessories (wheelchair etc.) and may be duplicated.

For those interested, it is possible to purchase the doll pattern with directions separately for $3. Other "New Friends" materials available include slide/tape programs, trainer's notebook and buttons with the "New Friends" logo.

When ordering add 10 percent of the order to cover postage and handling (special rates for large orders on request).

For more information or ordering, write to:

Chapel Hill Training-Outreach Project
Lincoln Center
Chapel Hill, NC 27514

Two other resources dealing with the acceptance of people who are different are **Hal's Pals** and **Special Kids Make Special Friends**.

Hal's Pals

Promoting an image of independence for children with disabilities is the goal of Mattel, a company that introduced a disabled doll line, **Hal's Pals**. The line includes: a ballerina with hearing aids, a girl with leg braces who walks with help from two canes, a boy dressed in a warmup suit and sitting in a wheelchair, a visually impaired girl with guide dog and cane, and a one-legged ski instructor.

The 19-inch, soft-sculptured dolls portray disabilities in a familiar, comfortable way, focusing on ability and strength, not pity, said Mary Doremus, director of the National Challenge Committee on Disabilities in **Child's Play** newsletter (June 1986).

For more information about **Hal's Pals**, write or call:

> For Challenged Kids
> Mattel, Inc.
> 5959 Triumph St.
> Commerce, CA   90840
> 1-800-227-3800

Special Kids Make Special Friends

"As part of our program, we are learning that each of us is similar in many ways and yet unique and special. A book that gives added dimension to this is **Special Kids Make Special Friends**," Merle Wynne, first grade teacher said. (Newbridge Road Elementary School, North Bellmore, N.Y.)

Special Kids Make Special Friends is published by the Association for Children with Down Syndrome. The clear, expressive photographs in this book capture special children with Down syndrome who are playing and learning in a preschool setting—sharing experiences with other children.

The text incorporates questions which involve the listeners and is suited for preschool and early grades. Through a pleasant story line young children can begin to gain an understanding of the meaning of handicapped and Down syndrome.

Special Kids Make Special Friends is available for $5 a copy (20 or more for $4.50). All orders must be prepaid.

To order, send request and remittance to:

> Association for Children with Down Syndrome, Inc.
> 2616 Martin Avenue
> Bellmore, NY   11710

Become aware of their differences in a positive way

Young children react differently to new situations. Some children will accept a disabled child without hesitation while the reactions of others will be mixed. At this stage the teacher should plan to discuss the handicap of the new student as well as other characteristics that make people different. Emphasis should be placed on the fact that we are all basically the same, yet special in our own ways.

It is important to encourage handicapped children to assist with work around the classroom. Many have a special skill such as sign language and should be given the opportunity to demonstrate it. In this way they will learn to cope with everyday activities and are perceived as being competent.

The way teachers arrange social interaction and plan learning tasks can help develop positive interaction between children. As children learn to cooperate they begin to see that each child can make a different contribution to the class.

"Young children will more frequently do what you do, rather than what you say to do," reminds Ms. Heekin. "Children will imitate your attitudes and behaviors toward differences among children." By creating positive attitudes toward differences, teachers can help children learn to accept and understand them.

Teaching Strategies

In early childhood classrooms various teaching strategies are needed. Each stage of young children's development has characteristic needs and behaviors. Being able to assess your students' actions and respond to their needs is a challenging role. The following articles will discuss methods and resources to help you teach cooperation, friendship and self-control.

Practical Guide to Solving Preschool Problems

It's morning activity time in the class for 5-year-olds and everyone is busy. In the game corner Justin is finishing a puzzle and Melissa is playing a matching game. Although each is involved in a quiet activity, you have mixed feelings.

You are pleased that Melissa is now capable of sitting for a short period of time and completing a task. Justin, however, spends all his time alone unless he is directed into a group activity where he is attentive, yet only occasionally participates. You're aware he has experienced family moves twice in the last year and has little experience in social interaction, but you had hoped that with gentle guidance he would have become integrated into the group. But after six months at school he still avoids social contact.

Many children, like Justin, are reserved when first entering a group setting. There are new situations and people to cope with, as well as the need to learn what is expected and what is appropriate.

Since it is difficult to reinforce Justin's social interaction, what is the best way to help him? One place to begin is reading **A Practical Guide to Solving Preschool Behavior Problems** by Eva Essa (Delmar, 1983). This excellent book provides practical guidelines to help the preschool teacher deal effectively with common behaviors that occur in most early childhood settings.

Once the specific behavior has been identified, Essa recommends observing the child for a few days, looking for possible clues to "when, where, how or why the behavior occurs." In Justin's case, she suggests asking questions such as:

> What does the child do instead of participating in social play or interaction?
> What does the child do when another child or children initiate interaction?
> If the child occasionally interacts with other children, who are they?

This assessment allows you to effectively see if the child lacks some of the social skills that help him interact or if he does not interact because he prefers adult attention.

There may be a simple solution. Essa has you look at alternatives. Does Justin need more time to adjust? Is he the youngest in the group—does he feel overpowered? Is it possible to place him in a more appropriate class?

Learning social skills is a goal

Because one of the main goals of early childhood education is to help preschool-aged children learn social skills, Essa feels children should spend at least one-third of their time during free-choice activities engaged in social play or interaction with peers. Her program for the child who does not participate in social play includes four stages:

1. Reinforce social interaction with other children.
2. Reinforce other children for interacting with the child.
3. Systematically teach social skills to the child.
4. Ignore the child when he does not interact with peers.
   The approach used for a particular child depends on the teacher's assessment of the cause of the behavior.*

She suggest that once you have talked to the parents and found, as in Justin's case, that the child has had little experience with other children his age or is shy around other youngsters, you can systematically help the child learn social skills.

The list of 40 chapters is extensive in **A Practical Guide to Solving Preschool Behavior Problems**. It covers almost any problem you might encounter, including hitting, disrupting group time, breaking toys, crying, clinging, whining, and nonparticipation. She has divided the book into seven sections: 1) Aggressive and Antisocial Behaviors; 2) Disruptive Behaviors; 3) Destructive Behaviors; 4) Emotional and Dependent Behaviors; 5) Participation in Social and School Activities; 6) Eating Behaviors; and 7) Multiple Problem Behaviors.

In her introduction, Essa provides an overview of social learning and explains, "Inappropriate behaviors exhibited by young children stem either from patterns that evolved in their past, or from a lack of understanding (caused by their limited social experiences) of what is expected of them. This is normal."

*Reprinted by permission from **A Practical Guide to Solving Preschool Behavior Problems** by Eva Essa, Delmar Publishers Inc., Copyright 1983.

The approach to effective guidance techniques is preempted by a short look at important factors affecting behaviors such as: Physical Environment, Child Development, Prevention, Rules and Consistency, Child's Concept of the Behavior, Frequency of Behavior, Teacher's Role, Home-School Communication, and the Setting.

All the chapters are presented in a standardized format utilizing observation, exploring consequences and alternatives, stating the goal and a step-by-step method for changing the specific behavior. Essa reflects that you may think it sounds like a lot of work, but points out that management of time resources is important. If troubling behaviors are not dealt with effectively, you will have to spend time and energy trying to cope with them.

A Practical Guide to Solving Preschool Behavior Problems is available for $13.95. For ordering information write or call:

Delmar Publishing Inc.
2 Computer Dr. West-Box 15015
Albany, NY   12212-5015
(518) 459-1150
1-800-833-3350
1-800-252-2550 (NYS)

Self-esteem Through Self-control

You're beginning a music lesson using lumi sticks. Everyone is settled, almost. Micah is crawling around bulldozing his neighbors and Patsy has run off, again, to play with the toys.

All young children are spontaneous at one time or another, moving and touching everything around them. However, there are children who seem to have an unusual amount of energy. They are continually restless, unable to keep their hands to themselves and unattentive.

It's important first to remember that at this early age your students are developing new control over their emotions, movement and communication. Lawrence Shapiro, author of **Games to Grow On—Activities to Help Children Learn Self-Control** (Prentice-Hall, 1981), points out that nearly everything preschool children do is an issue of self-control. The cognitive and behavioral skills they learn, such as increasing their attention and concentration span, acquiring impulse control and relationships with others, will be the basis for future development.

"While there are many other factors involved in success in school," continues Shapiro, "studies have shown that children who cannot control themselves are the ones who are most frequently identified as problems by their teachers, and who are prone to academic failure."

Self-concept goes hand-in-hand with self-control. If the child feels incapable of producing positive actions, he will not try. Thus, self-concept or self-esteem is often determined by how others perceive him and respond to him.

Games to Grow On provides activities to help children develop self-esteem through self-control. Shapiro helps adults understand the child's point of view, strengths and weaknesses and has made a list of principles to follow when working with the impulsive child. See "How To Relate While You Play the Game" which follows this article.

As children learn these new behavioral skills it is often necessary to point out their mistakes. Criticism can be more effective if they are intermittently praised or encouraged for their good behavior. Discipline integrates a teacher's skill to control a situation and enforce rules while expressing that they are unhappy with the poor behavior, not with the children. It's important when disciplining to stay calm. Children learn how to handle problems by observing other people, and will benefit by your control and understanding.

Children are individuals and will respond differently to a specific situation. Because of his behavior, an overactive child often receives a considerable amount of negative attention.

Significant behaviors of good learning

In his chapter on "Teaching the Preschool Child Self-control" in **Games to Grow On**, Shapiro looks at the most significant behaviors the child will need in order to be identified as a good learner in school: "the ability to sit for a reasonable period of time and the ability to work independently." He feels the most crucial thing to remember when working with a child is to choose an activity that is fun for both you and the child. Also, the activity should address the skill area in which you feel your child's development is lacking. By instructing the overactive child while that child is having fun, you can help him gain a head start in learning early school concepts and find ways in which he learns best. If you find Micah learns well through art activities—it can be an important diagnostic factor in his early school years.

By helping Patsy become more aware of her body movements, she may be able to control them more and overcome her difficulties. Ask her if she can move like a turtle or a broken car. Later, see if she's able to slow down her movements while doing a purposeful activity: "Can you carry that game to the shelf the way a turtle would do it?"

One of the most important things teachers can give young children is a positive self-concept and the ability to have self-control. With these attributes the child will have a more positive school experience.

How To Relate While You Play The Game

The relationship that the adult and child will establish is as important as the game you select. The following principles must be followed at all times in working with the impulsive child. Write them on a 3X5 card, and take this card with you whenever you work together. Read them **before and after** each activity, and try to correct the mistakes you make (don't worry, you **will** make mistakes, but the trick is to learn from them).

★ Principle 1. **Be Persistent:** Every effort must be made to complete a game. The message to the child must be: I will not let this go wrong; I will not let you fail again. If you find that it is difficult to complete games with the child, make them simpler so that they require less time.

★ Principle 2. **Try to Guarantee Success:** Always guide the child towards choices which will offer him or her success and rewards. Left to his own devices, the impulsive child with a poor self-concept will make choices that reaffirm his low self-esteem.

★ Principle 3. **Set Limits Clearly:** Make it very clear what is acceptable and what is not acceptable when you work together. While you must be able to tolerate the child's typically high activity level, you must not tolerate random destructiveness or aggressiveness. End the game rather than continue in frustration.

★ Principle 4. **Always Show Respect:** Respect everything a child is, and everything he does, and demonstrate this with your actions. Ignore the child when he devalues himself (but don't contradict him), and show him how you express pride in **your** accomplishments.

★ Principle 5. **Define Your Relationship as Positive:** Show the child through your actions and verbal statements that you value your time together. If you cannot do this with complete sincerity, then perhaps you are not the right person to be working with the child.

★ Principle 6. **Help Positive Decision Making:** Give the child choices that are clear and positive. Appropriate decision making is a skill that can be learned, so provide plenty of practice.

★ Principle 7. **Do Not Reinforce Maladaptive Behaviors:** Ignore inappropriate behaviors that the child is using just to get your attention.

★ Principle 8. **Give Social Reinforcement Often While You Play:** Reinforce your child every time he works for a long period of time, shows his motivation to learn, or succeeds at any task. You can do this naturally by giving him praise and affection, by your gestures, and by your body position.

Reprinted by permission from the book, **Games To Grow On—Activities to Help Children Learn Self-Control** by Lawrence E. Shapiro. © 1981 by Prentice-Hall, Inc. Published by Prentice-Hall, Inc. Englewood Cliffs, NJ 07632.

Games to Grow On is no longer in print, however you can obtain a copy of this valuable resource through interlibrary loan. Contact your librarian for further information.

Tug of War/Tug of Peace

"The rule of thumb for the neighborhood has been 'hit if you are hit,' no matter if it was an accident...Telling the children to talk it out and helping them to do the same has been consistently less than successful," said Dolores Schmitz of Milwaukee (Wis.)

"Children need more than chance opportunities to learn effective cooperation skills, more than praising good behaviors and punishing bad behaviors," she said.

In order to develop cooperation and decrease the number of aggressive acts among the kindergarten children during play time, Schmitz implemented a program in which randomly picked pairs of students worked on manipulative tasks together.

"Frosting Cupcakes" was one of the cooperative tasks created and described in her report, "The Design and Implementation of 40 Manipulative Tasks to Develop Cooperation in a Kindergarten Class at Palmer School." During this activity, child "A" received powdered sugar in a baggie, a spoon, 10 cinnamon red hots and a cupcake. Child "B" received milk in a small paper cup, a margarine bowl, four pecans and a cupcake.

By combining the materials and sharing their equipment, the frosting is made, and the cupcakes are frosted. Red hots and pecans are put on in a "one for you, one for me" pattern until all are used. The partners then go immediately to eat together, and then choose a play activity together.

"Friendship is built on the cooperation of two persons," Schmitz said. By teaching cooperative behaviors, the classroom becomes more fun, achievement is up and life outside school becomes happier, less aggressive.

The importance of this type of program, in which adults teach children to accept others and see the best in them while developing a relationship, was confirmed by Nel Nodding of Stanford University, at a California Association of the Education of Young Children conference.

In her keynote speech, "Caring at Home and at School" Nodding stressed the importance of developing a warm and caring environment so that children will become competent not only intellectually, but socially, emotionally and ethically.

Cooperation—A key to guiding children

A key to guiding children to help, share, and trust one another as well as work together is cooperation. By teaching cooperation, teachers can enhance children's self-esteem while fostering social awareness and responsibility.

William Kreidler, author of **Creative Conflict Resolution** found that there are two advantages when you teach cooperation. One is that academic performances often increase when cooperative activities are appropriately used and that there are fewer conflicts.

Interested in drawing your children into a more cooperative spirit?

"Changing classroom practices means simply establishing routines and procedures that encourage and reward cooperation," Kreidler said. "In the People's Republic of China, the children's clothing often buttons down the back. Thus, children must help each other dress and undress. Although some of us Americans are uncomfortable with that example, the point is worth heeding: if you want kids to help each other, give them opportunities to do so."

If you are continually plagued by untied shoes, have those students who can tie shoes do the tying. "They not only are more patient—they enjoy it more," Kreidler said.

If children need help on a project, it can often be beneficial to let them be assisted by their peers who are competent. A 4-or-5-year-old can often give clues toward the solution to a problem without giving the answer.

Do you have students who reject others' ideas or would sooner grab an object rather than share it when working in a group? Just as children learn other new skills, they need to learn how to cooperate. This includes learning communication skills which help them find words to express their feelings. As these skills are being learned remember to emphasize the pleasure they can gain by working with a group.

"You shouldn't be afraid to label cooperative behavior when it occurs," Kreidler said. "After all, we don't hesitate to tell a student that he or she did something 'all by yourself.' There are plenty of opportunities in classrooms to say, 'We did it together,' or, 'You did a good job cooperating.' Don't let these opportunities go by."

For small groups, a cooperative activity like "Monster Making" is excellent. The children can decide together what the creation will be and each one gets a chance to help make it. The nice thing about monsters or outer space creatures is that they can have several heads and only one foot and look 'just right'. After finishing the monsters the children can discuss what they like about them or make up a story to go with the monsters they made.

Developing class projects such as working on wall charts or preparing a simple meal are good ways to encourage a feeling of community in the classroom.

Cooperative games and activities

Cooperative games provide another way to practice cooperative skills. The group is challenged, they work together and everyone wins. Instead of hoping that others will be eliminated, as in a competitive game, the children can support each other.

In **Creative Conflict Resolutions** there are many good examples of cooperative games and activities including "Cooperative musical chairs." In this game the goal is for everyone to get a seat when the music stops. The difference, however, is that seats can be shared or laps utilized. If some participants fall off, the group starts again.

A challenging alternative to "Tug-of-War," is "Tug-of-Peace" where a rope is laid out in a circle. The object of the game is for all the members of the group to raise themselves to a standing position by pulling on the rope. This game, along with such stand-bys as "Balloon Bounce," where the group keeps the balloon from falling to the ground, or "Mirroring Images" brings the students attention toward working with others rather than against them.

Cooperative and competitive activities may both have a place in the classroom—sparking interest and creating a timely change of pace. One creates independent interaction while the other builds interdependence with the group.

Cooperative games are important, but they needn't necessarily replace competitive games, Kreidler said. "I look at cooperative games as a way of giving the other side—cooperation—equal time."

*Reprinted with permission from ERIC (226 845) "The Design and Implementation of 40 Manipulative Tasks to Develop Cooperation in a Kindergarten Class at Palmer School," by Dolores Schmitz. See "Young and Old Together" in the Volunteer chapter for ordering ERIC material.

Considerations for Social Growth

"Give me back my puzzle," 4-year-old Brian said firmly, pulling the game away from Duane.

That initial reaction to sharing is common among young children who are just learning that their peers have equally strong wants and needs, and often other points of view. To help children make sense out of their world, early childhood teachers need to be consistent and yet still responsive to the child's needs.

Fulfilling this role includes the teacher's ability to recognize there is a wide range of individual differences among children's sociability and that fluctuations in the intensity of children's peer relationships are normal, writes Charles Smith, author of **Promoting the Social Development of Young Children—Strategies and Activities** (Mayfield, 1982). Like adults, some children like to observe, rest and reflect on what is going on around them, Smith said.

He suggests that teachers talk with children to explore their ideas about sharing, associations and friendship, allowing a better understanding of the behavior. That may involve confronting a child's difficulty in understanding others' perspectives and misconceptions, which are often related to their developmental level.

One avenue suggested to help children produce ideas and resolve conflicts among their peers is to develop problem-solving skills. Before children are capable of using these skills, however, it is important for them to develop thinking and language skills.

Develop problem-solving skills

Knowing the difference between "why and because" or "now and later" is crucial to children's appreciation and understanding of the cause-and-effect relationship. One way to improve this knowledge of relational concepts is to extend language gradually into the future and past through the "planning process," writes Mary Hohmann of High/Scope Education Foundation. Talking about what the child has done and what the child will do, with whom, how and so on will help develop the spatial perspectives of conversations.

"We add a caution that this be done gradually and always in relation to a core of shared experience; this will help the child to master abstract concepts and become a better communicator and problem-solver," Ms. Hohmann said. (**Young Children in Action**, High/Scope Press, 1979, p.148).

Within a problem situation children are often unaware of other children's emotions. By learning to look and listen they can find out how people feel. Methods suggested to help children improve their self-concept, become aware of other people's feelings and learn to cooperate is discussed in Smith's book, **Promoting the Social Development of Young Children—Strategies and Activities**. It contains 100 personal/social skill activities for 3- to 5-year-olds, all with an emphasis on social development.

The activities are organized into five key areas: Body and Sensory Awareness, Emotions, Friendship and Affiliation (the ability to approach others and initiate relations), Conflict Resolution and Cooperation, and Kindness.

The format of each activity includes: a recommended minimum age for participants, purpose or target skills for the activity, setting, materials, and a step-by-step explanation of how to introduce and complete the activity.

Additional information deals with changes in personal/social development of children, providing in-depth understanding of the issues related to the skills. It identifies not only relevant personal/social topics, but also examines behaviors to be encouraged. "For example, we might emphasize the topic 'cooperation' in our classroom," says Smith, "but a goal of cooperation alone is not sufficient. We must decide what specific behavior or cognitive process we want children to learn."

Smith recommends that readers focus on skills and activities and includes perspectives to help teachers form a clearer picture of how they might implement their ideas.

Promoting the Social Development of Young Children—Strategies and Activities is available for $13.95, plus $2 for shipping and handling. California residents add 6.5 percent tax. To order, send remittance and name of publication to:

Mayfield Publishing
285 Hamilton Ave.
Palo Alto, CA   94301

A Peaceful Classroom: More Than Being Quiet

Children learn social skills, values, moral judgments, and intellectual and physical skills through play. Unfortunately, children seem to be patterning their play after television violence rather than traditional roles of family members and community helpers, according to Joe Frost, education professor at the University of Texas (Austin).

As a result of his findings—that 85 percent of the new television cartoons are war-oriented—he thinks it is important for parents and teachers to counter the focus on war and violence with an emphasis on peace.

"The point is, television is such a dramatic influence on children that it is difficult to help children tune it out in play," he said. "It's easier for children to learn war concepts, than it is concepts of peace, because war has concrete examples—violence, hit, maim, kill. Peace is abstract and is more difficult for young children to learn."

Developing a peaceful classroom is a primary goal of early childhood educators and most are well trained to create this environment. They have been encouraged to act and speak in a positive manner; deal with the behavior and not with the individual; and to meet needs on the level at which the child is functioning.

A peaceable classroom—A warm and caring community

A peaceful, cooperative classroom can suggest different things to different people. In the book, **Creative Conflict Resolution**, author William Kreidler explains that his definition of a "peaceable classroom" is not related to noise levels, class size, or open versus traditional teaching styles. It refers instead to a classroom that is a warm and caring community, where there are five qualities present:

1. Cooperation. Children learn to work together and trust, help, and share with each other.

2. Communication. Children learn to observe carefully, communicate accurately, and listen sensitively.

3. Tolerance. Children learn to respect and appreciate people's differences and to understand prejudice and how it works.

4. Positive emotional expression. Children learn to express feelings, particularly anger and frustration, in ways that are not aggressive or destructive, and children learn self-control.

5. Conflict resolution. Children learn the skills of responding creatively to conflict in the context of a supportive, caring community.

The strength of this model, Kreidler explains, comes from its interrelatedness...."that is to say, the whole is greater than the sum of its parts." In order to deal constructively with conflict situations, children need to gain insight into feelings and gain the skills of communication, cooperation and tolerance.

Anger is not the same as hitting

To help children develop positive emotion expression let them know that it is normal to feel anger and aggression and to have conflict. They also need to become aware, however, that they will have to learn to deal with these feelings in a positive manner and to resolve conflicts peacefully.

A teacher can accomplish this by sharing her feelings and explaining that feelings are different from the behavior often associated with the emotion, according to Charles Smith, extension specialist in Human Development at Kansas State University (Manhattan) and author of **Promoting the Social Development of Young Children**. "For example, anger is not the same as hitting and feeling afraid is not the same as running away," he says.

A teacher can show her disapproval of unacceptable behavior as well as acknowledge the children's feelings by talking to them and explaining they can "talk rather than hit," Smith said.

Children will feel more comfortable in sharing their feelings, if they know you accept them. This openness may also give you an opportunity to better understand the problem by learning more about their thoughts.

"If we view emotions as tools we can take time to understand their significance and learn how to use them best," Smith said. "By helping children understand what feelings are, how emotions originate, and what their consequences might be, we may contribute to their mastery of emotions."

Skills of effective communication

Although most young children are in an egocentric stage of development, they can begin to develop an understanding of emotions and start to empathize with others. Also, as language development takes place, young children learn to make their questions or desires clear so that others can understand them. This skill of effective communication is often encouraged through the use of puppets, dramatic play centers and team activities where it is necessary for the group to work together, such as making play dough or working on team puzzles.

Teachers interested in a larger variety of activities should read **Promoting the Social Development of Young Children**. It is an excellent source of strategies and activities which deal with emotions as well as empathy, affiliation (making friends), conflict resolution and cooperation.

The activities, developed specifically for young children by Smith, help children become aware of feelings and to understand the relationships between emotions and social behavior.

For example, in the activity, "Not Enough," children 4-years-old and older can learn to negotiate in response to conflict. The teacher tells a group of children that she has a problem they must solve. She then provides them with something which cannot be easily divided among all members (ex. five balloons). The teachers then says, "I would like to give you these things, but I think we might have a problem. What do you think it is?" After the children identify the problem (not enough to go around), ask for help to find a solution.

Smith suggests the teacher engage the children in a discussion about how the objects are to be given out. "Do not impose your solution, but try to have the children discover some mutually agreeable solution of their own. Try to see that everyone's ideas are discussed, and encourage the children to make their own decisions. Point out and discuss the inevitable disagreements that will occur. If the group cannot find a solution, the teacher can offer suggestions for discussion."

This activity was tried with 15 4-year-olds. They came up with these suggestions, Smith reported: Going to the store for more; not handing them out at all; cutting them in half (a humorous nonsolution); and for those who did not receive one, they would obtain one tomorrow, if the teacher found more that evening(p.194).

Focus attention on problem, not participants

As conflicts arise in the classroom, it is important to keep them from spreading and becoming violent, Kreidler said. To accomplish this, focus attention on the problem, not on the participants; attempt to decrease the exposed emotion and perceived threat; and help children learn how to make peace—or have someone help them to do so.

Helping children deal more effectively with each other and in conflict situations is also the purpose of Kreidler's book, **Creative Conflict Resolution**. It supplies more than 200 activities for keeping peace in the classroom. The activities are directed toward students in grades K-6. Many are very appropriate for kindergarten students, many of whom may becoming frustrated by high expectations, or are beginning to feel the pressure of competition and formation of cliques.

The activity, "Storytelling," from **Creative Conflict Resolution** helps children distance themselves from a conflict so they can discuss their behavior. An example is given describing how one teacher utilized this activity and insisted that her students spell exactly how sharing would take place.

When a conflict arises in the classroom, children need to realize that there are more options than just winning or losing—as portrayed in the media. By encouraging children to deal with their emotions, gain respect for themselves and others, and develop problem-solving skills for resolving conflicts peacefully, we will nurture their social development.

Creative Conflict Resolution is available for $10.95. For UPS shipping add $1 and add applicable state tax. To order, send remittance and title name and number (#15642) to:

Scott, Foresman and Company
1900 E. Lake Ave.
Glenview, IL   60025

See "Considerations for Social Growth" for ordering information for **Promoting the Social Development of Young Children.**

I Smile My Brightest Smile for a PAL

What will my teacher be like? Will I have a friend?

Entering a classroom and becoming part of a large group for the first time is overwhelming for many young children. They long to know that they belong and will have a "pal."

"Allowing children a part in setting up the room helps them feel the room belongs to them as well as to the teacher," according to Donna Denker, former Director of the Laboratory Preschool at Centenary College, (Hackettstown, N.J.). "Avoid having everything out and ready. They can help put flowers in a vase, start the record player, or even put finishing touches on the bulletin board."

Greeting each child at child's eye level with self-introduction, a smile and the PALS handshake is another method Denker uses to make entering the classroom a positive experience for the children. This routine, significant to her program, is a part of the CORE/PALS Learning Process which is based on developing the whole child/whole curriculum through developing friendships.

"CORE/PALS is a composite idea," said Gina Clare, creator of the program and presently associate professor of Education at Monmouth College (West Long Branch, NJ).

> The CORE stands for the basics—the essentials needed to survive and flourish... symbolized by the core of an apple. Its seeds represent knowledge which can emerge into robust, healthy fruit if properly cared for. And so it is with the mind of a child—the growth potential is enormous if we understand the proper cultivation process. A critical aspect of this nurturing, we feel, is a warm, compatible environment. Therefore, we have coupled with the CORE the idea of joint learning through friendships, or PALS.

The PALS "Greeting Song" is a simple example of the CORE/PALS philosophy. "When the children make friends in tangible ways through the handshake, eye contact and a smile, they learn to read and give direct signs of warmth and good will," Clare said.

The song is done with a different PAL in the classroom each day. A pairing system chart is used so it is possible for each child to pair with every other child in the class in a systematic and positive manner.

"It's important to do it every day," Clare said. "We develop good habits and attitudes through repetition, and set the stage for a positive environment of learning and cooperation."

Three special puppet friends help introduce and reinforce these pro-social attitudes and skills: Froggie (an idealist, believing all children can be friends), Mousie (a realist who needs to be shown how children can be friends) and Puppy (the spirit of the very young: great love for life but little self control).

Teaching respect for self and others

The CORE/PAL Learning Process is a structured method to develop cognitive, motor and social skills through the arts and in a friendly classroom. "Teaching respect for self and others and the environment is a basic attitude and enhances the climate of learning," according to Mary Lynn Mount, curriculum coordinator. "This in turn, increases instructional time, simply because of fewer disciplinary problems."

CORE/PALS also includes a "Spiral Curriculum in Social Studies," based on the song "We All Live Together" (Youngheart Music) which is a progression of concepts from the neighborhood to the whole universe. Another component is the "Rainbow Curriculum," a Home and School Learning Program that creates a mutual support system for the child's optimal development.

The components of the program, designed to include a large group, a small group and individualized learning, are used by teachers as a core schedule. However, it is possible to integrate the activities if there is a curriculum already prescribed.

As children master the basic skills in a friendly environment where they are learning, they become self-disciplined, confident and cooperative. "By having a PAL from day one," Mount said, "the child learns that there are other people in the world and that regard for others is important to daily life."

For more information on the CORE/PALS Learning Process, call or write to:

Uni-Ed Associates
Box 2343
Elberon, NJ 07740
(201) 870-0423

PALS' Greeting Song

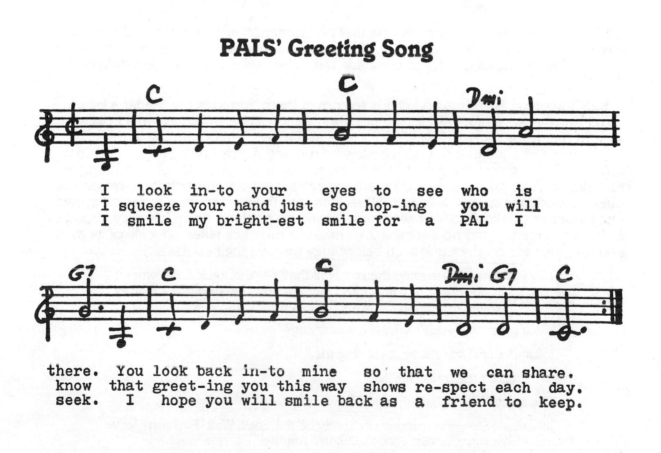

I look in-to your eyes to see who is
I squeeze your hand just so hop-ing you will
I smile my bright-est smile for a PAL I

there. You look back in-to mine so that we can share.
know that greet-ing you this way shows re-spect each day.
seek. I hope you will smile back as a friend to keep.

Reprinted by permission. Copyright by G. Clare, Arr. by T. DiRenzo, 1978.

"Superheroes in the Doll Corner"

If your New Year's resolutions included reading one new book this year, I highly recommend Vivian G. Paley's, **Boys and Girls: Superheroes in the Doll Corner.**

The book records how Ms. Paley consciously took time to observe the similarities and differences between the girls and boys in her kindergarten class. Her findings on the play patterns and fantasies of the children lead her readers to conclude that Mother Goose may not have been so far off. "The little boys in her class clearly have something in their background or makeup that makes them fidgety and rambunctious in a way the little girls are not."

By the time children are 5 or 6 years old, the doll corner is in its final phase, Ms. Paley said. The children seek new social definition for "boy" and "girl." "They search everywhere for clues, hoping to create separate and final images. Society supplies Barbie dolls and Star Wars, but the children invent equally interesting symbols by themselves," she said.

Teacher's tolerance—a significant influence

The fact that girls skip and boys run is more than a difference in play patterns. These characteristics can have significant influence on the children's education— depending on the teacher's tolerance for running and aggressiveness expressed in the fantasy play of boys.

"Sometimes I treat running as a natural phenomenon and at other times as the enemy. Mood, not logic, seems to be the determining factor. The children are aware of my inconsistencies and try to persuade me," she said. "If we whisper, then can we do it?"

Reading of her blunders and efforts to correct them, reminds the reader a bit of Erma Bombeck, yet it allows for greater appreciation to be self-critical in a positive way. In one instance, she takes a close look at the problem of running in the classroom and finds that the rules outlawing running discriminate far more against the boys than against the girls. In response, she decides on a controlled running experience. After taking the children out to see high school students perform on the outdoor track she makes a large oval track around the room with a series of arrows. The two rules established: one-way running and no pushing are quickly revamped to include no chasing and no shooting fingers. Soon the track takes on a life of its own and the boys are on the track even before they remove their coats:

> They become superheroes the moment they see the track. Even worse, the arrows are having a hypnotic effect. Certain boys have difficulty leaving the track because they keep following the arrows.
>
> "What's wrong, Teddy? Why are you crying?"
>
> "Johnathan is Dracula. He's chasing me."
>
> "Just step off the track, Teddy."
>
> "The arrow!" he sobs helplessly.
>
> "Johathan! Stop this minute! Let Teddy off the track. Wait. Everyone leave the track! We must have a serious talk this minute!"
>
> There is instant silence as the children respond to the note of near-hysteria in my voice. The boys are flushed and worried, unsure of what has gone wrong. I have asked them to do the impossible: separate running from fantasy without the structure of an organized game.

As with this example, Ms. Paley encourages the reader, throughout the book, to actively seek new ways of looking at children's behavior as well as consciously adapting new attitudes toward teaching.

Even if you haven't set reading a new book as a goal, I invite you to be captivated by Ms. Paley's encounters with her boys and girls.

Boys and Girls: Superheroes in the Doll Corner is available for $5.95 in paperback (shipping and handling $1.13) and $12.50 in hardback (shipping and handling $1.38). To order, send remittance and title of publication to:

University of Chicago Press
Att: Order Dept.
11030 S. Langley Ave.
Chicago, IL   60629

Do you often find you don't know where the day has gone? There just wasn't enough time to finish that special art project or necessary skill building activity. The authors of **Let the Kids Do It!** may have a solution for your problem.

"Let the Kids Do It"

"We have observed that teachers in the early childhood classroom were spending up to 75 percent of their time doing management tasks rather than teaching," report Norma Ziegler, Betty Larson and Jane Byers, staff members of San Antonio College Child Development Center.

In response to the discovery, they have written a useful book, **Let the Kids Do It!** (Pitman Learning, 1983). In the book, they describe how to set up a classroom environment to encourage student self-direction. This includes making sure children know where materials are stored by using shelf indicators as well as marking interest centers (which are basic to their program) with signs, posters or mobiles. By initiating this type of self-learning, teachers are freed from giving constant reminders about where things are located and how to use them, and gives them more time to interact in positive ways.

The use of indirect guidance guidelines and activities has many advantages. "Young children have difficulty listening to long explanations and understanding detailed instructions," the authors reported. An alternative is to utilize pictures, illustrations and symbols. "By associating words with symbolic representations and pictorial messages, children lay a foundation for reading skills," the authors said.

A teacher can introduce these pictorial messages best with basic symbols that represent actions the children use every day. An eye symbol can be used for see or look, such as in the science center where the teacher wants to point out a new flower.

By printing the word "look" beneath the corresponding symbol it helps children to see the correlation between symbols and words. If a second language is understood or used by the children, print it as well, the authors suggest.

Once the children recognize the action symbol and the representative word, add another word for the action. "For example, the picture of a hand could have the word 'touch' on it. Later, the words 'do' or 'feel' could be substituted...These words can teach that one symbol may represent more than one idea," according to the authors.

Symbol charts gain attention and interest

Putting two or three symbols together creates a symbol chart which can be used to gain attention and interest, to emphasize a point, to indicate a sequence, or to remind the children to do or not do something. A slash through a no walking sign can be made for a tricycle area, the authors suggest. Children may already by familiar with this type of symbol from observing similar signs along highways or at airports.

Symbol charts and arrangement clues are also easily adapted to the dramatic play center. In **Let the Kids Do It!**, the authors describe a variety of ideas for self-guidance and indirect guidance. For example, restaurant materials might be stored in a gallon ice cream carton covered with a menu. A box of aprons can be cued with pictures of a baker, nurse or carpenter.

Rebus charts can be substitutes for words

Pictures stories (rebus charts) are another means teachers can use to encourage children to become independent. These sets of pictures or messages can be substituted for words in recipes, directions for art projects or instructions for the use of equipment. By providing some guidance to the activity and allowing children to go at their own pace, they can learn to follow a specific sequence through a left-to-right, pre-reading experience without constant direct intervention from the teacher.

"The [rebus] charts provide a puzzle or mystery-like situation to solve," the authors report. "This is apparent by the expressions on the children's faces as you introduce the chart sequence."

Introduce rebus charts with a single-step rebus, such as washing your hands and then gradually introduce other charts for routines. The most simple charts have less than four pictures. More complex have several steps in a row.

Each level of rebus chart should be introduced slowly and the children should be given some explanation of the steps—periodic reminders will also be necessary.

Potato Print Insect

Take Potato | Dip into paint | Press on paper | Let Dry | Draw

"At first glance, it may seem an overwhelming task to make the rebus charts, arrange the interest centers, cue areas and materials, but please consider the end results of these projects," the authors say. "We are convinced the independent learners and doers of today are the independent thinkers of tomorrow."

For those interested in other materials utilizing symbol charts and rebus materials, the **Let the Children Do It—Book 2!**, contains more information and Makemaster patterns which can be utilized in the classroom.

Let the Kids Do It! is available for $7.95 and **Let the Kids Do It!—Book 2** is $10.95. Postage and handling is free with prepayment otherwise add $2 for each book. California residents add 6.5 percent tax. To order, send remittance and title of publication to:

Pitman Learning
19 Davis Dr.
Belmont, CA 94002

Parent Communication

Messages that need to be shared with parents can often best be understood when they are in written form. You can effectively state all the information needed about the topic at hand—without being rushed by last minute instructions or distractions. Another advantage is that parents not only have a chance to read the information, but they can keep it on hand for further reference.

In order for notes or letters to parents to be effective, they first have to be noticed and secondly, read. The appearance of your communique conveys more than the stated message—if it is displayed attractively, it will show parents that you felt they were worth your extra time and attention.

Creative Parent Communication

Creative Parent Communication, a 45-page book that contains reproducible letter shells on which teachers can add their own notes or letters, was designed to assist you in this important task.

The letter shells highlighted with silhouettes of young children, quotations about childhood and graphic art from the NAAHE (National Association for the Advancement of Humane Education) can relay messages dealing with specific areas of the curriculum such as: science, nutrition, art, safety, health, classroom activities, reading, and social development, as well as letter shells for common situations such as invitations to the classroom, rainy-day procedures and daily schedule changes. There are also letter shells designed to be used for special messages to individual parents describing positive accomplishments and for interstaff notices.

Included in the introduction are reproduction instructions and a list of suggestions for improving parent communication. For example:

> For parents who receive the answer, "I don't know" to their question, "What did you do in school today?", a note with "quizillating questions" may be the answer. Quizillating questions are questions you can provide which relate directly to activities and materials covered during the day or week. For example, If you have been studying shapes, suggest that the parent ask a related question such as: "Can you find any rectangles in the kitchen?"

At the end of the book you will find a parent handout on monitoring children's television viewing and a selection of extra clip art and headings that can be used to create your own "noticeable notes."

Creative Parent Communication—Graphics Art for Teachers' Notes is available for $7.95, plus $2 for shipping and handling. To order, send request and remittance to:

> Pinnaroo Publishing
> P.O. Box 7525
> Bend, OR 97708

Another common and effective method of communicating with parents is through a newsletter. It can provide a perfect medium to let parents communicate with the teacher. One way to allow parents to give feedback on class plans and activities is through a "comment" section. By introducing it at the beginning of the year, parents learn it is an opportunity for them to suggest guest speakers, recommend field trip ideas or make other comments.

Happiness is Starting Right with Parents

Illustrations for the newsletter are often available from young artists in the classroom. If optional material is needed, however, there is an excellent supply of small clip art from the National Association for the Advancement of Humane Education (NAAHE).

The Miniature Menagerie: A Portfolio of Humane Education Clip Art (HE 1028), includes ten 10"x11" sheets containing animal illustrations by various artists, and helpful how-to instructions on its use. These appealing illustrations are ideal for placing on announcements, student activity sheets or enlarged for use on bulletin boards.

The portfolio is available for $4, or $3 for NAAHE members. To order, send publication number and name with remittance to:

> NAAHE
> Box 362
> East Haddam, CT 06423

Often there are important messages you wish to communicate to parents dealing with the needs of the whole child. Encouraging parents to monitor their children's viewing habits is a family matter which is a concern of many teachers. The amount of viewing time, in addition to the content of of what children watch, is important because this viewing time displaces more important creative, physical and social activities in their lives.

☜ "I Have a Headache This Big" ☞

Hearing this statement come from my 3-year-old son resparked my interest in the influence television has on young children today. We all see the effects of television on children in the classroom. In one week, a teacher may learn from her students that: there was a 'super' dinosaur special on TV; Mr. Rogers had a good recipe for playdough; a 'whole bunch' of new Christmas toys are now available; and the A-Team was scary.

Television exposes children to an extended view of their world. It can broaden their vocabulary, knowledge and interests. It can also, however, give them a distorted view of the world filled with vulgarity and violence. As Ron Powers, of CBS's "Sunday Morning" program reported, television has introduced us to a "universal language of guns" where people use guns and bullets to relay messages to one another.

It is this subject of violence on television and its relationship to children's aggressive behavior that causes concern for both parents and teachers, and has been the subject of hundreds of studies. Most often the findings show that children who watch violent television programs may become more fearful of the world around them and more likely to behave in an aggressive manner.

Television is here to stay

Whether we like it or not, television with its negative and positive aspects is here to stay and will continue to influence our students. A question raised by Bernadette Angle, Ph.D., Associate Professor at Youngstown State University, in her article, "We are What We Watch" (**Network**, April 1985) is: "How can we best help our students and their families use television as a learning tool rather than be used by it?"

Clarifying the difference between reality and fantasy

Encouraging parents to monitor their children's viewing habits and if possible, take time to watch programs with them is vital. By being available, parents can give children the opportunity to talk about what they've seen on television and convert passive TV watching into an active language and learning activity. They can also help clarify the difference between reality and fantasy and discuss program and commercial content. Making time for discussion at home (and in school), can allow children the opportunity to express their feelings be they the fears of robbers or the wonderment of a volcano.

For parents wanting to give their children early alternatives to television, Ms. Angle encourages them to read to their young children. It is important to foster an interest in reading at an early age. "If a child has a positive attitude toward reading, he or she will read regardless of television competition or other outside activities," she said.

Creating alternatives for television viewing is probably the most favored option for parents, but they may not always be successful. To assist parents in using television to help, not harm their children, Ms. Angle has made a list of suggestions. (See following page).

9 Ways to Use TV to Help, Not Harm, Your Child

1 **Don't use TV as a babysitter.** It may seem easier to place children in front of the television regardless of the quality of programming when you are busy around the house, but remember, children build strong family ties from their participation in household chores and shopping. Include them in these activities.

2 **Carefully select the shows your family watches.** Be the parent and insist that certain shows are off limits.

3 **Set aside a time for "family shows," programs you watch together.** When parents and children express views about the program's content and exchange ideas, family members gain insights about the program and each other.

4 **Include children in family decisions about what you will watch together.** This shows children their ideas are respected and can set the stage for family meetings to discuss other family projects.

5 **Be a model for your child.** Choose carefully the programs you watch.

6 **Don't use TV as a reward or punishment.** As such, it can become a crutch which places too much value on the medium. Instead, try to think of something more directly tied to the child's behavior.

7 **Join with other parents in your community to press for more and better programs for children and families.** Organized viewers do make a difference. You may also want to contact the national advocacy group Action for Children's Television, 46 Austin St., Newtonville, MA 02160.

8 **Use activities like the following to enhance the learning value of the TV shows you watch as a family :**

● Ask your child to exercise his/her imagination and think of another title for the program or series you are watching.

● Read newspaper articles together describing the show before watching it. Have your child write a description or narration of the program after viewing it.

● During a commercial break ask your child to predict what will happen next.

● Turn off the volume but leave the picture on. Ask your child to guess what is happening by watching the action without the sound.

● Have your child draw a picture describing his feelings about a show. Discuss the picture together.

● Ask your child to time the commercials during a show then add them together.

9 **Be as selective with your child's TV diet as you are with what he or she eats.** Just as we are what we eat, to some extent; so too we are what we watch!

Reprinted by permission by Bernadette Angle, Ph.D., Associate Professor at Youngstown State University, Special Education Department.

New Communication Tools

Have you ever considered pamphlets or brochures as a way to share information with parents? This method of introducing new topics and giving material to parents which they can refer to, is an effective way of strengthening home-school relationships.

These written communication tools can serve a variety of purposes, according to Michael L. Henniger, author of "Involving Parents Through Written Communication," (**Dimensions**, A Journal of the Southern Association on Children Under Six, Vol. 12, No.4):

> They can, for example, inform parents of valuable information on child growth and development. Other pamphlets and brochures are available on health and safety tips. Booklets on selecting toys for children and how to support the school through activities in the home are also plentiful. In addition, governments and schools publish materials that describe goals and objectives for education at all levels.

Why utilize this type of publication when you already communicate with parents through letters, notices or newsletters?

Henniger reminds us that it is just as important to use a variety of communication tools with parents, as it is to use a variety of teaching techniques with children: "Each parent is a unique individual with special needs, interests and preferences. In order to 'reach' each of these individuals, a variety of techniques (including written communication) should be used."

Pamphlets and brochures are available from governmental agencies, private businesses, and school related organizations and others. To help you become aware of what local or state publications are available, you might ask your state extension agent, local child services department or librarian.

A listing of various child care publications directed toward parents follows. It is advisable to write the order on your school letterhead to qualify for school discounts when applicable. It is also recommended that a check or money order accompany your order, although most will accept school purchasing orders. For shipments destined outside the United States, write to the company for shipping charges. Most materials will be delivered in three to six weeks.

Food Before Six

This eight page booklet (0005) for parents of 1-to 6-year-olds, is full of practical suggestions for helping children enjoy eating. It is available from your local Dairy Council, or write to:

National Dairy Council
6300 North River Rd.
Rosemont, IL   60018

Meal Planning for Young Children Ages 1-6 (45¢)*

This twenty page brochure offers guidance in understanding children's eating patterns, their likes and dislikes and their food needs. It also deals with how to handle such common situations as dining out and traveling with young children. It is available from:

General Mills, Inc.
Nutrition Dept.
Box 1112, Dept. 45
Minneapolis, MN   55440

My Child's Health Record (25/$6.25 minimum)*

This brochure provides parents with a method to maintain a history of their child's vision and dental examinations as well as a record of immunizations and other pertinent health care information. It is available from:

Auxiliary to the American Optometric Assn.
243 N. Lindburgh Blvd.
St. Louis, MO 63141

*Larger quantities available at a discount. For more information write the supplier.

Getting Involved

In many centers and schools there is a special section of the entryway or room where parents can learn of announcements; leave messages or requests; meet other parents and teachers; and dress or undress their children.

A bookshelf or table in this area with resource materials on parenting and child development is often well received, especially if the materials are available for lending. A valuable series of booklets, **Getting Involved** (U.S. Department of Health and Human Services), are designed for use by teachers interested in informing parents of the importance of play and how they can encourage their children to learn skills in an enjoyable way through everyday activities.

The **Getting Involved Series** includes:

Your Child's Attitude Toward Learning (GPO Stock #017-092-00087-1) ($2.25)
Your Child and Problem Solving (GPO Stock #017-092-00085-5) ($2.25)
Your Child and Reading (GPO Stock #017-092-00086-3) ($2.25)
Your Child and Language (GPO Stock #017-092-00089-8) ($2.25)
Your Child and Play (GPO Stock #017-092-00084-7) ($2.25)
Your Child and Math (GPO Stock #017-092-00081-2) ($3)
Your Child and T.V. (GPO Stock #017-092-00088-0) ($2)

These booklets average 20 pages, include large print for easy reading and are illustrated with large black-and-white photographs. Each book begins with an anecdotal introduction and then explains how children learn about the subject, why it is important and how parents can help children gradually learn the skills involved through daily experiences.

Orders must be accompanied by a check or money order made payable to the Superintendent of Documents. The orders must also include titles and GPO stock numbers. There is a 25 percent discount for 100 or more copies of any publication sent to one address.

To order, send remittance to:

Superintendent of Documents
U.S. Government Printing Office
Washington, D.C. 20402

Two other resources providing parents and teachers with information about child development and parent-child relationships are **Positive Parenting Booklets** and **Once Upon a Mind** parent education program.

Positive Parenting

"If you praise children for acting in ways that you approve, they are more likely to repeat their actions...Your approval spoken or unspoken—can make a world of difference."

These statements are found in **Praise Your Children**, an excellent booklet written for parents, explaining that praise is a way to guide children's behavior while helping them to feel good about themselves, about their abilities and about the things they do.

It is one of the **Positive Parenting Booklets** series from the Southwest Educational Development Laboratory. The booklets, designed to reach a multicultural audience, "help supply the information parents need to better understand the part they play in their children's development."

Each booklet, filled with expressive photographs, deals with a specific parenting topic and offers realistic suggestions. The average length is between 10-20 pages and the material is written on a 6th-7th grade level, making them easily read and appropriate for busy parents.

All the booklets do an excellent job of increasing the awareness of positive parenting practices and would be worthwhile reading for anyone working with young children.

In **Help Children Cope with Frustration**, parents are informed that children need to understand that there are good and bad ways to express what they feel. The book gives suggestions on how to help children learn to control their feelings by talking out problems and how parents themselves can help their children cope with their frustrations by setting a good example.

Being Consistent is a booklet as well as a growth wall chart. Children are supplied with a collection of animals to color and parents are provided with reminders on being consistent such as:

> Children like knowing what is expected of them. If you are consistent with your children, it will also help them learn to limit their own behavior. And knowing that you love them—even when they make mistakes—helps children feel secure. Remember, be consistent.

Other booklets in the series are:

Children Learn by Watching and Helping
Expect the Best from Your Children
Four Ways to Discipline Children
Los Ninos Aprenden Mirando y Ayundando
(Bilingual—on how children learn)
Pay Attention to Your Children
Read to Your Child
Talking with Children
Where Do Adults Come From?

The **Positive Parent Booklets** are available in quantities starting at a minimum order of ten copies; 10-500 copies at 60¢ each, and more than 500 copies at 55¢ each. Add 15 percent for shipping and handling. All orders must be prepaid.

For more information, or ordering, write to:

Positive Parent
Southwest Educational Development Laboratory
211 East 7th St.
Austin, TX 78701

Why do children eagerly await storytime? This response is due to the fact that children relish that special moment when a person gives them time and attention, according to Charles A. Smith, Ph.D, an extension specialist in Human Development at Kansas State University (Manhattan).

Once Upon a Mind

Smith is co-author with Carolyn Foat, an educational psychologist of a Kansas parent educational program, **Once Upon A Mind**. Program goals are to use children's literature to provide parents and caretakers with information about child development, to strengthen parent-child relationships, and to help children learn personal and social skills.

They describe some specific storytime objectives helpful for teachers and parents:

More effectively integrate storytime into the classroom's daily schedule;

Become familiar with guidelines for evaluating the quality of children's books;

Identify ideas or values you believe are important to convey and discuss them before or after reading to the children;

Use stories to enhance children's understanding of themselves and others and nurture their effective personal and social behavior.

The program is centered on a $2 handbook entitled, **Once Upon A Mind: Using Children's Books to Nurture Self-Discovery**. The handbook includes guidelines for choosing, introducing and reading books to children, in addition to short reviews of 81 recommended books geared toward 3-to 8-year old children. There are also ideas for discussing the themes and characters, and activities for incorporating the books' concepts. Some of the themes covered are Cooperation, Fear/Courage/Security and Friendship/Belonging.

Also available are back issues of the **Once Upon A Mind Quarterly** newsletter ($3/yr.), which addresses a particular theme in each issue. Smith provides valuable insights on the subject covered, as well as lists recommended books and suggestions for related talks and activities.

1983 Quarterlies and Study Guides: Sibling Relationships, Courage/Fear, Sharing/Giving, and Sex Education.

1984 Quarterlies and Study Guides: Divorce/Separation, Anger, Sadness/Loneliness, Conflict and Violence.

1985 Quarterlies and Study Guides: Imagination/Fantasy, Compassion/Love, Communication/Honesty, Death/Life.

Prepaid orders and requests for information should be sent to:

Once Upon A Mind
Extension Home Economics
343 Justin Hall
Kansas State University
Manhattan, KS 66506

Parents are busy people, yet they want and need to know what goes on at school. They also appreciate teachers providing up-to-date information on child development which allows them to participate more fully in their child's education. Using a variety of written communication to share this information can be an asset to building a meaningful parent-teacher relationship.

Classroom Volunteers

Is she reliable?

Who will prepare her to work in the classroom?

These questions are normal. They stress the importance of planning a volunteer program. The following three books can help you answer these questions and assist you in determining what your needs are and how to involve volunteers effectively into your program.

Initiating a Volunteer Program

An excellent book designed specifically for those interested in initiating, updating or evaluating a volunteer program is **Educational Volunteerism** by Susanne E. Taranto and Simon O. Johnson (C. Thomas, 1984). It is a comprehensive guide which provides a list of proven, practical, easy-to-implement activities for new or experienced volunteers.

Taranto and Johnson point out a "needs assessment" is vital to provide information to develop the program's goals and objectives. By discussing with your teachers their needs and expectations you can write job descriptions, including responsibilities and hours. Interested volunteers can look them over before deciding if they want to offer their services. You will also become aware of tasks that require specific training.

The job or task made available should convey usefulness and provide the volunteer with personal achievement. By considering the skills and interest of the volunteer and matching them with teacher expectations, you will increase the chance for a successful program.

Volunteer coordinator monitors the program

It is recommended by Taranto that a "volunteer coordinator" is available who can monitor and coordinate the program. This job would encompass recruiting, orientation, scheduling hours and activities and answering questions which arise. Because you may not have the time or expertise to serve as coordinator, you may want to contact a volunteer office in your community for help in providing you with a person to develop and maintain your program or help to train someone to fill this position.

Educational Volunteerism includes a chapter which lists 25 activities proven useful to volunteer programs which may serve as motivational tools.

After the volunteers have been chosen, it's important for them to feel a part of the program so that they can effectively fill their role. An orientation period should be planned to explain expectations in the area of discipline, location of supplies, emergency procedures, etc. Taranto and Johnson have found that one way to encourage teachers and volunteers to work as a team is to allow them to participate together in an orientation inservice. Questions and concerns can be discussed and procedures developed for conflict resolution. By soliciting feedback throughout the year from the teachers **and** the volunteers, the program will become most efficient. It is stressed that a volunteer program must be a "dynamic ongoing process" that is constantly undergoing evaluation.

Teachers who have the help of another adult often find it is easier to have activities well organized and meet the needs of their students. Through this cooperative effort, it is possible to increase the student instructional strategies for both the teacher and the volunteer and create opportunities that will allow student motivation to increase.

To order **Educational Volunteerism**, send $14.75 (postage paid when remittance is sent with order) to:

Charles C. Thomas Publisher
2600 South First Street
Springfield, IL   62717

Join the Team

Welcome to the world of volunteers and aides!

This positive statement introduces you to an exciting handbook, **So You Want to Join the Team**, written for volunteers, aides, cooperating teachers and administrators.

Authors, Dale Brubaker and Molly James Sloan, do an excellent job of preparing both the aide and the teacher in understanding what is involved in cooperative teaching. They discuss the need for cooperative decision making in curriculum planning and implementation, as well as effective classroom management. A real benefit, they point out, is the opportunity for each team member to step back and see events in a different way—influencing the learning of the children and adults involved.

Communication is more than talking, the authors explain. It is thinking, feeling and acting so that we better understand ourselves and are in turn better understood by others.

Often we find it difficult to listen to each child's stories when other children need attention. "This is one reason why aides and volunteers are such an important part of the classroom," affirm the authors. "You can help the teacher listen."

In the chapter on "listening", pitfalls for listeners are identified and examples of how aides can learn from their experience is shown. One such pitfall is that of the listener being so interested in what they are going to say next that the sender feels the message isn't even hear:

> ...Aides and volunteers tell us that they have to remind themselves to give children a chance to respond. One volunteer said: "At first I was so interested in covering a story or activity that I didn't really take time to listen to the child's messages. With time I learned that it didn't really make much difference if it took twice as long to read a story. The child wanted to make the story his own by adding things to it." This volunteer had learned a significant thing, active listening improves interaction between adult and the child and makes teaching less teacher-centered and more communication or interaction centered.*

The book concludes with a chapter on "Individualized Learning," stressing the importance of flexibility and observing the uniqueness of each learner in the classroom. In this section, as in the rest of the book, the use of anecdotes livens the text and "brings home" those situations which commonly appear in a cooperative-teaching environment. A valuable resource for volunteers, aides and teacher for $13.95.

To order, send remittance and name of publication to:

Kendall/Hunt Publishing Co.
2460 Kerper Blvd.
Dubuque, IA   52001

*Reprinted from **So You Want to Join the Team**, by Dale Brubaker and Molly J. Sloan. Copyright 1981 by Kendall/Hunt Publishing Co. Used with permission.

Special Ways to Say "Thank You"

On your clipboard (under the stack of notes) you have a long list of jobs to accomplish. The list seems to grow daily. But there is hope, you've just completed the woodworking center with the help of Mr. Jackson, Valerie's grandfather, who is a carpenter.

Today Mr. Jackson has asked if he could visit the class again and work with them in other ways. It sounds like a good idea since you both work well together, but you feel you could use some guidance in just how to orient him to your classroom procedures and the best ways to evaluate him.

Effective Involvement of School Volunteers, a 22-page handbook from the National School Volunteer Program (NSVP), was also written to help teachers learn to involve school volunteers creatively and effectively in educational programs. In addition to covering basic information on orienting volunteers to the classroom it contains seven useful appendices: Ways Volunteers Can Help; Sample Teacher Request Form for Volunteer Services; Initial Teacher/Volunteer Conference Checklist; 25 Ways to Show Appreciation To Your Volunteer; Self-evaluation for the Volunteer and for the Teacher; Some Definitions Drawn Up by NSVP/NEA Task Force; and Guidelines for a Teamwork Approach to a School Volunteer Program.

Maintain volunteer morale

One unique concept developed was how to show continuing appreciation for the volunteer's service. The volunteer's "pay," explains editor Dorothy Mulligan, is often the wide smile of a child when he or she sees the volunteer arrive, a picture "that I made just for you," or the warm day-to-day relationships with the teacher, other staff members and volunteers. However, the students and teachers with whom the volunteer comes in contact can do much to maintain volunteer morale.

Mulligan suggests a teacher should prepare children for the volunteer who will work with them by building a positive attitude toward the volunteer's contribution. "The teacher should encourage children to call the volunteers by name and to show their appreciation by giving notes and cards on birthdays and holidays when they are ill or absent," she notes.

Volunteers will feel more like partners on the educational team if they are involved in staff meetings, inservice training or planning sessions when they can benefit from the program.

Mulligan learned of a special way to say "thank you" in West Chester, Pennsylvania. Here the volunteers who gave regular service for five or more continuous months received a card which admitted them to all school sponsored activities, including high school sports events and plays...

Other methods of sharing appreciation are found in the appendix of the handbook. Some of these are:

> Share articles and books of mutual interest—on child development, learning styles or content area in which the volunteer works.

> Nominate your volunteer for a volunteer award.

> Commend the volunteer to supervisory staff.

> Write an article on the volunteer's contributions for your volunteer newsletter, school newspaper, or community paper.

> Give the volunteer increasing responsibilities and more challenging tasks—enable the volunteer to grow on the job.

Effective Involvement of School Volunteers is available for $3.30 (VA shipment add 4 percent sales tax). No C.O.D. orders accepted. For more information, or ordering, write to:

> NSVP
> 701 N. Fairfax St.
> Alexandria, VA 22314

Young and Old Together

Few volunteers walk into the class uninvited. Letting parents and members of the community become aware of your requests is vital. As a result of their requests, many teachers are finding there are a great number of highly productive and knowledgeable older volunteers capable of passing on their skills and experiences to young children. With this knowledge, large numbers of intergenerational programs are being established which are directed at strengthening communications between senior citizens and the young. The reasons for taking advantage of this talent pool are varied.

Children benefit from the opportunity to learn something special from their new friends and the exposure to a wider variety of classroom experiences. The volunteers can create a tighter bond between the school or center and the community. They can speak on behalf of the children and become their advocates.

Understanding and Respect for the aging

One of the most important benefits is the personal growth associated with interacting with the elderly and the additional support they provide. Because of the accelerated mobility of the 1980s and the dramatic changes in family structure, contact between children and their elders has become limited. This has lead to fewer mutually enriching encounters, which lessens the development of positive attitudes between the old and young generation.

By utilizing these volunteers the children receive more individualized attention and develop special relationships. Also, through a positive, personal association, the child can gain understanding and respect for the aging process.

When the older volunteers share their gifts of interest, skill and wisdom a feeling of usefulness is fostered. However, it is important to remember to provide possibilities for their personal achievement and growth. This allows for continued enthusiasm by the participants and insures a more successful program.

A practical document for those interested in developing an intergenerational program is **Young and Old Together: A Training Manual for Intergenerational Programs,** by Carol Seefeldt (1979). It is available through most university libraries and the ERIC system (Doc. No. Ed. 210 089).

ERIC is a nationwide information system funded by the National Institute of Education and is designed to make information on all aspects of education readily available. To order a copy of this ERIC document (paper or microfiche), write for an order form from:

ERIC Document Reproduction Service
Computer Microfilm Corporation
3900 Wheller Ave.
Alexandria, VA   22304
(800) 227-3742

By exploring your own neighborhood you may find a talent pool of older persons interested in sharing their energy and unlimited skills. In most communities there are state or local volunteer offices from which older volunteers can be recruited. They may also be able to help establishing a "volunteer coordinator" needed for an effective volunteer program.

If your position is that of director, it is important to determine if your staff would welcome contributions of older adults. Teachers must know that their work load will not increase substantially because they have agreed to use a volunteer and understand they have been oriented in the school's program and procedures. For the program to be successful, the staff involved will need to have genuine respect for the older volunteers and view them as valuable contributors to the education of their children.

Another way to retain volunteers is include them in evaluation of the work you do together. "...but don't bother to evaluate if you don't plan to use the results to improve performance," notes Mulligan of NSVP. This is true when working with any volunteer—parent, retiree or high school student.

Training and Evaluating Student Volunteers

Preschool and day care administrators are often approached by home economics teachers to see if they might accept high school students as volunteers. When accepting, administrators must realize that they are accepting a certain amount of training responsibility. The intensity of the training required will depend, in large part, on the background the student has obtained through previous Child Development courses.

Donna Johnson, the Child Development teacher at Redmond High School (Redmond, OR), runs a community preschool through the high school. Her teaching and evaluation method of her students are worthy of emulation.

First she presents an introductory session of Child Development. There she stresses the importance of teaching and the responsibility involved. She wants her students to realize that "we all parent kids."

Following the session, her students spend time rotating through the three distinct positions of teacher, volunteer aide and planner. By filling all three roles, the students are able to understand the problems and pleasures of different aspects of teaching—here they can find their strengths and weaknesses. Johnson recommends this type of experience for teaching student volunteers so they can become aware of all aspects of the teaching role.

Johnson utilizes an "Employee Performance and Work Appraisal" form for evaluating her student volunteers, which she finds to work extremely well. Her students are able to use if for future reference when applying for work at preschool/day care facilities or for nanny positions. A copy of this form follows.

For Use with Student Child Care Workers

Name of Student _____ Employer _____ Date Report is Due _____

TO THE EMPLOYER: It will help the school in planning future training for the student worker if you complete this report. Please read it carefully. On each line, place one check mark over the phrase which describes the worker most accurately. If you think the individual is about halfway between two descriptions, make your mark about halfway between them on that line. Any additional comments you wish to make will be helpful.

Date _____ to Date _____, Coordinator _____ High School _____

1. Ability to follow instructions	Seems unable to follow instructions	Needs repeated detailed instructions	Follows most instructions with little difficulty	Follows instructions with no difficulty	Uses initiative in interpreting and following instructions
2. Ability to get along with people	Frequently rude and unfriendly — uncooperative	Sometimes lacks poise and understanding — seems indifferent	Usually gets along well with people	Usually poised, courteous, tactful in working with people	Unusually tactful and understanding in dealing with all types of people
3. Attitude toward appearance of work station	Maintains careless, slovenly work station	Allows work station to become disorganized	Follows good housekeeping rules	Takes pride in appearance and arrangement of work	Keeps work place outstandingly neat and efficiently organized
4. Cooperation	Uncooperative, antagonistic — hard to get along with	Cooperates reluctantly	Cooperates willingly when asked	Usually cooperates eagerly and cheerfully	Always cooperates eagerly and cheerfully without being asked
5. Industry	Always attempts to avoid work	Sometimes attempts to avoid work	Does assigned job willingly	Does more than assigned job willingly if given directions	Shows originality and resourcefulness in going beyond assigned job without continual direction
6. Quality of work	Does almost no acceptable work	Does less than required amount of satisfactory work	Does normal amount of acceptable work	Does more than required amount of neat, accurate work	Shows special aptitude for doing neat, accurate work beyond the required amount
7. Dependability and Judgment	Unreliable, even under careful supervision	Sometimes fails in obligations even under careful supervision	Meets obligations under careful supervision	Meets obligations with very little supervision	Meets all obligations unfailingly without supervision
8. Appearance	Slovenly and inappropriately groomed — disagreeable personality	Sometimes neglectful of appearance — ineffective personality	Satisfactory appearance and personality	Neat and appropriately groomed — pleasing personality	Exceptionally neat and appropriately groomed — outstanding personality
PROGRESS	Fails to do an adequate job	Lets down on the job somewhat — slow to learn new techniques	Maintains a constant level of performance	Shows considerable progress — learns new techniques reasonably fast	Shows outstanding progress — learns quickly
OVERALL ESTIMATE OF STUDENT'S WORK	Poor	Below average	Average	Above average	Outstanding

Suggested Grade: A B C D F COMMENTS: _____

Days absent _____

Days tardy _____

Signature of Student _____ Signature of Employer or Supervisor _____

142

Administration

Meeting Your Special Needs

The school year has begun in earnest—teachers and students are becoming familiar with classroom schedules and rules. Well, almost. Yesterday, Dade kept climbing up the slide backwards while Kathy, a new teacher, was on duty, and Molly wandered off each time Sue, an aide, watched her class.

How can you help staff members become better able to cope with daily classroom situations when there is a shortage of time and money for teacher training?

Planned learning experience

A "planned learning experience" is one option to consider. As described in "Where to Find Training," (**Texas Child Care Quarterly**, Fall 1985), this type of training session can be conducted by the director and is useful in approaching specific needs of the entire staff or of selected individuals. The director identifies the objectives, the activities, ways to evaluate what was learned, and follow-up activities.

Advantages of this program include the director's opportunity to initiate it around the staff's schedule and utilize a variety of sources, beginning with a review of the director's own policies.

In the area of discipline there are many articles which can be used for discussion. One example is, "Dealing with Difficult Young Children—Strategies for teachers and parents," by Anne K. Soderman (**Young Children**, July 1985). It covers children's individual temperaments and recommends ways to understand and build upon children's strengths. Copies can be made to share with teachers if you receive the journal, or you can order a single copy of the article for $2 from NAEYC, 1834 Connecticut Ave. N.W., Washington D.C., 20009.

Other informative and reasonably priced publications that could be used are:

A Guide to Discipline by Jannette G. Stone (NAEYC, 1983)—This is an easy-to-read book about teaching children to respect themselves and others and to show that respect. It discusses the development of children's self-esteem, ways to talk to children and questions, such as, "What can I do in advance to avoid problems?" and "What do you do when children run around the room, knocking into people and things?" To order this 32-page book, send $2 and request for publication #302 to NAEYC, 1834 Connecticut Ave. N.W., Washington D.C.

Discipline is Not a Dirty Word by Jennifer Birckmayer (Cornell Cooperative Extension, 1984)—A workshop outline for parents and teachers, this booklet gives guidelines for discussion leaders and focuses on seven principles of discipline, including "working with children instead of against them," and "offer children choices only when you are willing to abide by their decisions." Also, there are practice episodes for teachers of young children which show how all seven principles work together. To order, send $2.50 with name of title, order number HDFS 51, and number of copies to Distribution Center C, 7 Research Park, Cornell University, Ithaca, NY, 14850.

Participants can apply what they've learned

Besides discussing the information presented, the participants can plan to apply what they have learned in their classroom. Other possible activities could include having them share their findings with other members of the staff.

An evaluation can be initiated by asking participants to explain how they would handle particular classroom discipline situations. A follow-up activity could involve implementing a change in the classroom environment to encourage better behavior.

The success of this learning experience is best measured by the way in which the participants use their new knowledge or skills within their classrooms. With proper planning and presentation and interesting and useful resources, this on-the-job training can become an excellent way to help the staff improve its self-esteem and teaching skills.

New Application for Child Guidance Program

Bea Ganson, Executive Director of the Day Nursery of Abilene (Texas) has found a new way to cope with the continuing need for staff training.

By utilizing the curriculum material, **Child Guidance for Child Caregivers** and **Nutrition, Health, and Safety for Child Caregivers** (Home Economics Curriculum Center at Texas Tech University), she has found a valuable tool with which she can train teachers, substitutes, aides and even the cooks.

Teaching strategies are varied

"An advantage of this program is the ease in which it may be used with these different groups," Ganson said. Designed to be used with post-secondary students (with a wide range of ages, educational background, academic abilities and reading levels), the teaching strategies are varied. They include: group discussion, posters, charts, games, lectures, role playing and others.

"These materials, which include both a teacher's guide and student lab manual, supply a great deal of valuable information and guidelines for teacher training sessions," Ganson said. "As executive director over three centers, I discuss with the directors what areas need to be covered and then we pull out those instructional units that are applicable from the curriculum."

Relating selection of guidance techniques to language development, discussing the effects of group patterns on young children and coping with undesirable behaviors, are but a few of the large selection of topics covered in the Child Development manual.

Each unit of the instructor's guide includes performance objectives, references, suggested classroom experiences, unit tests, and transparency and handout masters. Each unit of the student's guides include an overview, references, observation and participation lab experiences, and participation evaluation forms.

Material used in correlation with other text

The Curriculum Center staff notes that for effective utilization of these materials, they should be used in correlation with other texts on child development and related topics. Both guides include a bibliography and give references listed at the beginning of each unit, as well as a glossary of terms.

"As part of our training program, we have materials available to our teachers for reference. In each classroom there is also a notebook in which our office supplies new information on child development and curriculum," Ganson notes. "Evaluations of the teacher training sessions are done by the center's directors. For example, Anna Lara, one our directors, goes in and observes and evaluates her staff members. From these observations she can see what areas the teacher has improved on and those areas that may benefit from further training."

Ganson has shown that this curriculum program, though designed for use by post-secondary child development instructors, can be adapted to a director's training needs. With its large selection of teaching strategies and reasonable price it can be beneficial to directors who are looking for staff training guidelines.

For more information or order form, write to:

> Home Economics Curriculum Center
> Texas Tech University
> PO Box 4067
> Lubbock, TX   79409-4067

For day care directors who are in need of qualified substitutes, the practical experience of the Coastal Bend Child Care Adminstration Association may prove to be a solution.

New Way to Train Substitutes

It's 8 a.m. and, as director, you've gotten the 4-year-old class settled into its routine. Then, for the second time today, a teacher tells you she is sick and must go home.

Picking up the phone—again—you call a neighboring center to see if they know of a trained substitute who might be available.

How can this common problem, the lack of well-trained substitutes, be solved? The Coastal Bend Child Care Administrators Association of Corpus Christi found one answer may be a special, 12-hour, non-credit course for training substitutes, according to Linda Gifford in the **Texas Child Care Quarterly** (Winter, 1985).

Based on local directors training needs

The course, based on survey results of the local director's training needs, was developed by a task force led by Edna Jackson and the Early Childhood Specialist Department staff at Del Mar College.

"The course covered information on child growth, child abuse, releasing children to parents, guidance, emergencies and state minimum standards. Participants obtained a food handler's certification, job references, TB test results, and documentation of training," Ms. Gifford said.

The administrators association, led by Edna Jackson, recruited students from child care centers and from the general public, and then reimbursed the cost of the training to the 28 people who completed the course. A list of their names was then distributed to participating child care centers.

The substitutes found the course very useful and allowed them to become aware of what to expect from directors in terms of support and written activities. The training class was so successful that the association has repeated it numerous times, Ms. Gifford said.

Information packet available

A packet describing the development of the course is available for $5. It contains the history and process of the project including: 1)Recruitment and costs, 2) Course outline, 3) Needs assessment, and 4) Maintenance of substitute list.

To receive the information packet, send request and remittance to:

Glenda Stanton
YWCA
4601 Corona
Corpus Christi, TX   78411
(512-857-5661)

Directors of day cares, preschools or kindergartens often have similar needs. Besides providing teacher training, they must: do comparative shopping; be prepared to handle emergencies; and know how to advertise their facility. Surviving this onslaught of technicalities dealing with children, parents, teachers and school policies is discussed next.

Reduce Costs and Save Time

It is not uncommon for teachers or directors to do comparative shopping for new equipment or other materials. Unfortunately, it is often time consuming to find values.

Louise Child Care (Pittsburgh, PA) has found a successful way to save time and money by utilizing bulk purchasing. In the fall of 1981, the program directors began researching alternative plans to develop a bulk purchasing service that would be offered to local child care providers. "We studied the information gathered on the best available prices for furnishing the infant/toddler center [a new pilot program], plus information collected concerning costs of pre-school equipment and supplies, paper products, office supplies and cleaning materials." Jane Fulton, director of the program, explained. "The recommendation that followed the evaluation of our purchasing practices was that we investigate the possibilities of buying in bulk from a limited number of companies at specific times during the year," she said.

Bulk purchasing is cost effective

The program directors believed purchasing in bulk could be beneficial and would offer the following advantages to child care providers:

1) The cost-effective use of staff and supplies.
2) Staff time spent with vendors, many of which are not used, is greatly lessened.
3) Louise Child Care handles the administration of the purchasing.
4) The bottom line is the ability to purchase quality goods at a savings.

At a meeting with the local Daycare Association, a survey was distributed which assessed their needs and available suppliers. A tally of the survey listed the preferred companies that were cost effective.

Initiating a purchasing service

In March 1982, with the encouragement of the Association, Louise Child Care's bulk purchasing service was initiated. Ms. Fulton describes its progression:

"The service began with two vendors, one for pre-school equipment and the other for infant/toddler equipment. Four organizations, including Louise, participated in the first order of $3,451.56. In July of 1982, nine groups ordered $6,429.77 worth of equipment. The orders and the number of participating organizations have increased each time until we now have orders of between $20,000 and $30,000 per quarter and 53 organizations using the service.

Two other vendors have been added—one for consumables and office supplies and one for cleaning materials and paper products. The discounts range from 15% to 40% and include free shipping. Louise Child Care charges an administration fee of 5% of the total order.

Louise Child Care accepts bids from vendors once a year, usually in the fall. Bids are evaluated by a committee of child care providers and the bulk purchasing staff of Louise as to the quality and variety of the products, base price, delivery and return policies of the company, and the discount offered.

Recruiting participants is important

The process of recruiting participants is an important part of this bulk purchasing service. "You can't just change the way people order materials," Fulton said. By utilizing monthly postcards, they encouraged members to first place a small order, thus introducing them to the service. "Once people sit down and try it, they realize the money they saved," she said.

A newsletter was also a means to keep members informed of products and procedures. "You have to think of ways communication can help you—it is important to keep your customers happy," Fulton said.

A smaller scale of this bulk purchasing program was initiated in Grand Rapids, Michigan by Pat Ward and Bonnie Negen of the Steel Case Child Care Service Corporate Programs.

The one-year pilot program was begun with funding by the local AEYC. Designed to help the broad community, it was utilized by child care centers, preschools, small family day care providers and other groups.

"We were a catalyst in the community," Ward said. Directors and providers were encouraged to take advantage of this cost-effective and time-saving method of obtaining materials. They ordered four times a year and paid a small cover charge for administrative fees.

A purchasing coordinator was hired on a part-time basis, rather than having the job held by a staff member. The coordinator was able to work out of her home and use her garage for storage, Ward said.

Keep communication open

"Besides dealing with the ordering and fulfillment of goods during the quarterly periods, it is vital to keep communication open," Ms. Ward said. At one time a 16 page monthly newsletter kept members up to date with purchasing information. A procedure they found useful was arranging to have their mailing list taken to a computer company. Labels were made with the zip codes presorted which simplified the bulk mailing procedure.

The existence of written communication is only one reason for the necessity to having funding for the program, Ward said. A group starting a bulk purchasing service needs to take into consideration the cost of publishing the newsletter, postage and a bulk mailing permit. In addition, there is the cost of office supplies, purchasing coordinator's salary and possible office and storage space, she said.

At the end of the first year, the Kent County 4-C took over the program with the backing of another local grant. Groups taking advantage of this service are required to be a member of the County 4-C's. The service provides quality merchandise at a reasonable price for all members and is particularly valuable for smaller facilities and home care providers which would not otherwise be able to purchase these materials, Deb VanverMolen, program director said.

If you have questions or would like more information write:

Jane Fulton
Louise Child Care
336 S. Aiken Ave.
Pittsburgh, PA   15232

Plans to Prevent Panic

A volcanic eruption near Anchorage caused a daycare center to comply to an air pollution alert. A freak explosion at a refinery endangered a child care center in Houston. A hurricane alert caused a preschool to close near Boston.

Emergencies and the possible hazards connected with them vary according to locality. However, a standard rule is not to panic. This is best accomplished if there are well-designed emergency plans which describe what to do, when to do it and how it should be done, according to **Texas Child Care Quarterly** editor, Linda Gifford, in her article "What Would You Do in an Emergency?" (**Texas Child Quarterly**, Vol.9, No.3).

Where can you get assistance to make these plans?

"Local school districts and nursing homes may already have plans that directors can review as a first step," Gifford said. Other excellent sources of information are the local fire inspector and the American Red Cross as well as personnel from Civil Defense and Emergency Management Offices.

Directors and teachers can check their emergency preparedness by answering the questions below, Gifford said.

1. When the building must be evacuated, is a certain person designated to take the emergency medical forms and emergency contact information for each child?

2. Do the children and adults practice techniques such as feeling a closed door before opening it, crawling low to avoid heat and poisonous gases, and doing the stop-drop-roll drill if they catch on fire?

3. Do several people know how to cut off the electricity, gas, and water to the building?

4. In case the center must call for emergency help, has someone written complete directions detailing the fastest route to the center and posted them near the telephone?

5. If the center has to be evacuated because of a flood or tornado, would parents know where to go to pick up their children? *

If a director scored five yes answers to these questions and has clearly written plans covering all possible emergencies, the children will be in capable hands if an emergency arises. Everyone hopes no one will have to use these plans in a real emergency. But being prepared for emergencies is the only way to deal effectively and safely with them.

For those located in a hurricane zone and who need emergency guidelines, Irma Woods, child development specialist with the Texas Department of Human Services in Corpus Christi, has written a sample for the area's child care directors.

It includes emergency phone numbers (for that area), defines hurricane stages and outlines hurricane preparedness. This is clearly divided into four areas of responsibility—administration, physical plant (administrative assistant), food service, and entrance and exit to the building.

The plan is available for $1. To order, send request and remittance to:

Corporate Child Development Fund for Texas
510 South Congress, Suite 122
Austin, TX   78704

* Reprinted by permission from "What Would You do in an Emergency?", **Texas Child Care Quarterly**, Vol. 9, No. 3.

Need answers to other legal and administrative problems? Read on:

The Child Care Law Center

The park, post office, or McDonalds? Field trips involve much more than deciding where to go.

Is your vehicle insurance coverage adequate?

Will you need to insure private cars driven on behalf of the program?

Find the answers to these and many other important questions in **Property and Vehicle Insurance**—one of the various publications developed and distributed by the Child Care Law Center.

The Center, located in San Francisco, states the purpose of their publications is to "provide preventive law information to the child care community and inform them of legal issues in child care. Many of the publications respond to specific legal concerns which arise in the everyday operation of child care programs. Others offer a legal analysis of broader policy issues."

The Child Care Law Center is designed to help develop affordable, quality child care programs. It serves as a legal resource for the local, state and national child care communities. It offers educational seminars and a legal resource bank, in addition to technical assistance through a network of cooperating volunteer attorneys.

> Child Care Law Center
> 625 Market Street, Suite 915
> San Francisco, CA   94105

Managing the Media Maze

Many teachers and directors take a break from curriculum planning and take time to think of long-term goals—for their classroom, and for local early childhood education overall.

Various ECE groups may gather to discuss plans for local conferences directed toward educating the community on the assets of early childhood education and support for local teachers. Some may be organizing a large fund raiser, while others in the child-care field may want to impress on the public that they are committed to improving child care services.

Utilize local media

A valuable resource for all three groups is a booklet, **Managing the Media Maze**, published by the Child Care Employee Project. By providing incentive and practical suggestions for approaching local media, the authors, Jane Friedman, Gerri Ginsburg and Marcy Whitebook, help teachers and directors utilize local television, radio and print media which can be intimidating to those who are unfamiliar with them.

By educating themselves about the media and being organized and strategic in their approach, staff members can find access to media is less time consuming and expensive than they might think, the authors say.

Designate a "media representative"

One of the first steps discussed in the booklet is the designation of a "media representative" knowledgeable about the school's or center's program and a person who can effectively relay information. Once this is accomplished it is important to decide on focus and the format that best serves the facility's needs.

The next step is to develop a "Media Book" which is your resource file of local media. It becomes your guide and reference with the necessary information in case you need to publicize an event or contact the media for any reason.

Other areas covered in **Managing the Media Maze** are: "Making News," "Specific Skills for Working with the Media," "Media Options," "Getting Positive Results," "Evaluating Your Efforts," "Resources," and "Sample Press Releases."

Managing the Media Maze is available for $2.50 plus 50 cents for postage. To order the booklet, or for more information on relevant materials regarding improving salaries and status of child care, write:

Child Care Employee Project
PO Box 5603
Berkeley, CA   94705

Survival Kit for Directors

Do you wish you had a "Mary Ellen's Best Idea Book for Directors" to help you cope with the daily challenges and frustrations you meet? The Early Childhood Directors Association of St. Paul, Minnesota, has answered that call with their helpful handbook, **Survival Kit for Directors**.

Learning how other directors deal with inappropriate use of staff sick leave, scheduling substitutes, and receiving feedback from the silent majority (parents) are but a few ideas discussed in the first two sections, "Staff Management" and "Planning and Organizing."

Effective ways to solve problems

In the following four sections, "Children," "Communication," "Policies and Tuition," and "Environment" you can read of effective ways to solve such problems as: children spitting, A.M.-P.M. communication, acknowledging donations, parents' misunderstanding of policies, and coping with costly paper products.

A specific incident is stated for each problem as well as a description of "How was it solved?" "Steps in implementation," and "Comments." (See following)

The combination of fresh, new insights along with common solutions make this book a valuable resource for ECE directors who are looking for ways to make their job a bit easier.

The **Survival Kit for Directors** is available for $5.95 plus $1 for postage and handling. (Minnesota residents add 6% sales tax.) To order, send request and remittance to:

Early Childhood Directors Association
906 North Dale Street
St. Paul, MN   55103

Problem Solving for Supervisors

PROBLEM AREA: **LACK OF PROFESSIONAL RESOURCES**

SPECIFIC INCIDENT:

A teacher wanted some books on discipline to help with a problem, but the center didn't have the ones she mentioned and couldn't afford to buy them.

HOW WAS IT SOLVED?:

A library was set up using books that staff members were willing to bring in and share.

STEPS IN IMPLEMENTATION:

1. Many teachers had purchased various books of their own and were frequently bringing them in for each other anyway.

2. The staff decided to formalize the system and encourage people to bring in books to establish a professional library for the teachers.

3. The staff wrote their names in their books and turned in a master list of the books they loaned to the library. A sign-out sheet for the books was used and a two-week limit for check-out was established. A shelf of reserve books to be used only in the center was also established.

COMMENTS:

The library was put in the staff lounge so people could browse through books on breaks or at naptime. A kitty of contributions and fines for late books was initiated. The money is used to purchase books for the center and to replace any books that get lost. People have been very responsible about taking care of the books and really appreciate having them available. This system does a lot for professional development and morale in the center.

PROBLEM AREA: **SCHEDULING PART-TIME CHILDREN**

SPECIFIC INCIDENT:

Parents were constantly asking if their child could come on Wednesday instead of Tuesday this week or make other changes in their schedule.

HOW WAS IT SOLVED?

A paired partner system for all part-time children was developed so that parents negotiated with each other. That made each family responsible for the portion of a slot for which they had enrolled their child. This helped meet the parents' need for some flexibility without putting the added burden on the staff.

STEPS IN IMPLEMENTATION:

1. After registration, a letter is sent to each family confirming their child's schedule.

2. Parents sign a contract to pay for the days and times for which they have enrolled their child.

3. If one child attends Monday, Wednesday, and Friday and another attends Tuesday and Thursday, the two families are considered to share on full-time slot and can negotiate any changes between themselves.

4. Parents are informed in writing of the family with which they share a full-time slot.

COMMENTS:

If parents want to switch the days their child attends, they contact each other and arrange a trade, eliminating the need for the director to be involved in juggling bookkeeping or checking for room. All part-time children "share" their slot with another child and the parents are made aware of their partner. Parents making a switch are requested to send a note to the teacher letting her know. To implement this system part-time parents are now asked how flexible their schedules are and it is noted on their forms. An attempt is made to match people who need or want flexibility.

Reprinted by permission from **Survival Kit for Directors** (Early Childhood Directors Association)

Index

Illustration Credits

"Square," from **Sesame Street Activities**, p. 3, by Jane O'Connor, Children's Television Workshop. Page 11

"Bird Bird," from **Sharing the Street-Activities for all Children**, p. 25, Barbara Kolucki, Children's Television Workshop. Page 12

"Sleeping Grump," from **Sleeping Grump** game, Family Pastimes and Animal Town Game Co. Page 15

"Computer Center," from "Set Up a Computer Play Center," **Texas Child Care Quarterly**, Vol.8,No.2. Page 17

"Stamps," from the Great American Wallflower Co. Page 28

"Snack time," from "Nutrition Activities: Preschoolers and Parent, p. 14, **Early Childhood Nutrition Program**, by Jill Randall and Christine Olson, Cornell University. Page 32

"Vegetable garden," from **Menu for Mealtimes**, p. 7, M.L. Bader, S. Feinberg, C.J. Ullo, Middle Country Public Library. Page 37

"Tiger Beetle," from **Coloring Fun with Insects**, Entomological Society of America. Page 42

"Sharing Sam," from **Humane Education**, National Association for the Advancement of Humane Education. Page 45

"Sea shells," from **Seashore Curriculum Unit**, pp. 16-17, by Patricia Stillwell, Bay Area Association for Education of Young Children. Page 46

"Offalot," from **Offalot** Energy Program, Energy Source Education Program. Page 47

"Wastey Watts," from **The Adventures of Mini-volts and Wastey Watts**, National Energy Foundation. Page 49

"Natural gas," from **Natural Gas Storybook**, National Energy Foundation. Page 50

"Don't Put Anything in Your Ears," from **Healthy Hearing Poster**, National Association for Hearing and Speech Action. Page 54

"Scrubby Bear," from **Scrubby Bear** Handwashing Poster, Scrubby Bear Foundation. Page 56

"Curb," from **Preschool Pedestrian Safety Program**, by Janice Sutkus, Illus. by Janet LaSalle, National Safety Council. Page 62

"Walkers have to see the street," from "I Listen and Look for Cars Coming," **Early Childhood Traffic Education-2**, p.7, American Automobile Association. Page 64

"Girl at corner," from **Traffic Safety**, American Automobile Association. Page 65

"Water safety," from **Safe at Home**, p.81, American Lung Association of Los Angeles County. Page 67

"Tele-Photo Phone Book," cover of **Tele-Photo Phone Book**, Mother Goose Distributing. Page 73

"Hug-A-Tree," from **Hug-A-Tree and Survive** Handout, Hug-A-Tree and Survive. Page 75

"Indian doll," from **Daybreak Star Preschool Activities Book**, Daybreak Star Press. Page 81

"Jackrabbit and sun," from "Jackrabbit's Hunting Trip," **Literature from Indian Country**, Celia Totus Enterprises, Inc. Page 82

"New Friends," from **New Friends** Teacher's Guide, Chapel Hill Training Outreach Project. Page 97

"Creative Parent Communication pages," from **Creative Parent Communication**, Pinnaroo Publishing. Page 125

"Ground hog," from **Miniature Menagerie: A Portfolio of Humane Education Clip Art**, National Association for the Advancement of Humane Education. Page 126

"We'll put your sweater on over your shoulders," from **Discipline Is Not a Dirty Word**, p.6, by Jennifer Brickmayer, Cornell Cooperative Extension. Page 146

Remaining illustrations from **Preschool Perspectives-The Monthly Newsletter for Early Childhood Educators**, Pinnaroo Publishing. Pages 13, 24, 34, 70, 80, 88, 91, 92, 96, 104, 106, 109, 111, 113, 114, 119, 121, 136, 138, 139, 141, 148

Related Publications

Use this form to order additional copies of **Early Educators Tool Box**, or other related publications.

Early Educators Tool Box   /$12.95/

Creative Parent Communication—Graphic Art for Teachers' Notes

An easy and attractive way to share news with parents—**Creative Parent Communication** provides you with graphic letter shells on which to write your notes and announcements. Eye-catching graphics encourage two-way communication and are an asset for more effective teacher-parent communications. Make your notes noticeable!

/Removable and reproducible/Promotes Professional Image/$7.95

Preschool Perspectives—The Monthly Newsletter for Educators of Young Children

Keep up-to-date on new developments in Early Childhood Education without taking time to wade through lengthy publications by reading **Preschool Perspectives**—the award winning newsletter.

A valuable companion to activity oriented publications—**Preschool Perspectives** covers a variety of topics on Child Development, Early Childhood Education and Resources. Yet, its concise, non-clinical articles will allow you to keep informed despite your busy schedule.

/Subscription newsletter—1 year/10 issues/$18.00

Gold Award winner *"for overall excellence"* — 13th Annual Newsletter Award Competition, Washington, D.C., June 1985

⌐ **Creative Parent Communication** .... $ 7.95

⌐ **Early Educators Tool Box** $12.95

  (Please add $2 for postage and handling for one book, 50¢ for each additional book)..................._____

⌐ **Preschool Perspectives** $18.00

⌐ **Preschool Perspectives** Binder............. $ 6.95

  Total Enclosed ...._____

Name_____

Address_____

City_____ State_____ Zip_____

Mail to: **Pinnaroo Publishing**
         P.O. Box 7525
         Bend, OR 97708